The Bichon Frisé

Other books by the author

A Dog-owner's Guide to the Yorkshire Terrier
A Dog-owner's Guide to Poodles
The Dog Directory Guide to the Bichon Frisé

The Bichon Frisé

E. JACKIE RANSOM

Photographs by Marc Henrie

H. F. & G. WITHERBY LTD

First published in Great Britain 1990
by H. F. & G. WITHERBY LTD,
14 Henrietta Street, London WC2E 8QJ

Acknowledgements

The picture of Princess Charlotte of Wales and Lioni on page 13 is
reproduced by gracious permission of Her Majesty the Queen.
The Breed Standards are reproduced by kind permission of the Kennel
Club and American Kennel Club.

British Library Cataloguing in Publication Data
Ransom, Jackie
   The Bichon, frisé.
   1. Bichons Frisés. Care
   I. Title
   636.72

ISBN 0 85493 193 7

Typeset by CentraCet, Cambridge
Printed in Great Britain by St Edmundsbury Press Ltd,
Bury St Edmunds, Suffolk

Contents

Introduction

Deux boutons de bottine
Un morceau de charbon
La face enfarinée
'Je suis clown'.

This verse, from an unknown source, sums up the face and character of the Bichon Frisé we know today. Two black boot buttons, a touch of charcoal and a floured face certainly give them a resemblance to a clown in traditional make-up. Their ability to perform tricks, their enchanting and amusing character and happy disposition, smallness combined with strength and stable temperament make them a marvellous breed to own.

The alert, lively expressions of these Bichons Frisés typical of breed.

Their ability to perform tricks of their own devising is quite incredible. Any plaything, be it a ball or stick, will produce quite amazing feats, tossing the plaything in the air is often followed by a complete somersault. Bichons Frisés can jump many times their own height from a standing position, and their habit of standing on their back legs pawing the air makes it easy to understand how, for many years, they were considered clowns and circus dogs.

The advantages of this breed as pets are many: they do not shed their coats on clothes or furniture and they are good house dogs, although quiet at other times. I have yet to meet a bad-tempered Bichon Frisé. They are easy to train and, with kindness and patience, they will learn all that is required of them. To look its best a Bichon Frisé must be kept clean and well groomed. This requires a certain amount of time, but the reward is great. The striking appearance of a well-kept Bichon Frisé carrying its tail gaily over its back brings forth many complimentary remarks and of course the inevitable query 'What breed is that beautiful dog?'

1 History of the Breed

Through the ages the Bichon Frisé has given pleasure to many people, from aristocrats to street traders and circus audiences, filling each role with charm in keeping with their enchanting personality and temperament.

It is said that Cleopatra owned several of these little white dogs, and that their image can be found on Egyptian sarcophagi. Inevitably, however, the breed's early history is uncertain. It is probably descended from the Barbichon group of dogs, which is considered to consist of four categories: the Maltese, the Bolognese, the Havanese and the Teneriffe. The Teneriffe, or lap-dog of the Canary Islands, is thought to be the Bichon Frisé we know today.

THE MALTESE
The Maltese is a very ancient breed: Strabo, writing around AD25, called the breed Canis Melitei. In 1791 Buffon in his *Natural History* calls the breed Canis Melitaeus, describing it as common on a Mediterranean island but not necessarily indigenous to it, and closely related to the Bichons of northern Europe and the lap-dog of the Canary Islands.

In *The Dog*, published in 1872, Idestone wrote of the Maltese that 'a woolly coat is also found but the silky glistening hair is the only coat allowed'. Perhaps the woolly ones were the first Bichons Frisés. Idestone's description of the weight, length and type of coat, with black eyes and nose, face short but not chubby, tallies closely with the modern Maltese.

THE BOLOGNESE

The Bolognese also has very ancient origins, dating back at least to the 11th century. Known for its grace and beauty, it originated in the Italian city of Bologna, from which it gets its name. In the past centuries it was often depicted in paintings as black and white; although the many porcelain dog figurines modelled by J. J. Kaendler of the Meissen factory in the early 18th century show the Bolognese as having very heavy tan markings.

In the 11th and 12th centuries Bolognese dogs were held in great esteem for their fine hearing and abilities as guard dogs, despite their small size. In the 16th century the Duchess d'Este took with her from Italy a pair of Bolognese dogs as a present for Philip II of Spain. In his letter of thanks Philip wrote: 'Nothing more beautiful could be offered as a gift for a king'. Catherine Empress of Russia in the 18th century used to breed Bologneses. Madame de Pompadour (1721–1764) on asking her courtiers for a present, was presented with a Bolognese, a breed which consequently became extremely popular with the entire court of Louis XV.

The story that Cosimo dei Medici of Florence (1389–1464) owned several Bolognese dogs is substantiated by a painting from the school of Andrea del Verrocchio of the Angel Raphael and Tobias with a little white dog of this breed, painted during Cosimo's reign. Indeed, Bolognese dogs were so highly esteemed by Cosimo that he sent eight of them to Belgium to be given to a high ranking citizen of Brussels in his name. These days although the breed is still quite rare, the Federation Cynologique Internationale's (FCI) Standard for the breed is far longer and more detailed than that for the Bichon Frisé.

As the Bolognese appears to be closely related to the Bichon Frisé, the following is a brief attempt to pinpoint the main differences in the two breeds, which is no easy task even with the help of Fiorenzo Fiorone's *Encyclopedia of Dogs*, the standards in which are all compiled with the collaboration of the FCI. The Bichon Frisé Standard is about

360 words long, whereas the standard for the Bolognese is very much longer with about 2000 words, making it one of the longest in the book. In comparison with the Bichon Frisé the Bolognese is a very serious dog, not vivacious, and devoted to its owner almost to a point of abnegation. It has long hanging ears, set on high above the zygomatic arch, with the upper part standing out from the head giving the head a broader look. The muzzle is half the length of the skull, the eyes are deep ochre and coat flocked. All these requirements for the Bolognese are contrary to the standard for the Bichon Frisé but are still found in many of our Bichons today. It is surely not inconceivable that over the years the two breeds have been interbred, making the completely pure-bred Bolognese or Bichon Frisé a rarity.

A 19th-century engraving showing what is clearly an early type of Bichon on the left.

THE HAVANESE

The Havanese's history is obscure. There are two theories, one is that the Bolognese was taken from Italy and crossbred with a small Poodle, creating a new type of Bichon called by the Cubans the 'Havanese'. The other theory, advanced by the 19th-century naturalist Dechambre, is somewhat different. In his opinion the Havanese was descended from the Maltese, taken to the West Indies by the Spaniards and called the Havanese Silk Dog. A different opinion is expressed by

Dr Fernand Mery in his book *Le Chien* published in Paris in 1959. He considers that the Havanese came from France and was the largest of the Bichon family, but not over 14 inches at the shoulder, with flat, silky, very long hair. Of the coat's colour, Dr Mery writes that 'some authors claim the coat should be pure white while others say the Havanese is white, brown or beige, and that like the Teneriffe it is a Bichon that has returned to France after a long and involuntary exile'. However a recent article written by Dorothy L. Goodale published in the USA adds to our knowledge of the breed: 'The Havanese is longer in body compared to its height, legs short and straight, height from 8 to 10.5 inches at shoulder, coat profuse, wavy to curly. Colour shades of white, cream, gold, chocolate, blue, black or a combination of any of these. In all other aspects they are the same as a Bichon Frisé.'

THE TENERIFFE—THE BICHON FRISÉ
The history of the Bichon Teneriffe, or Canary Islands Lap-Dog, is difficult to trace. Juba, King of Mauritania, made an expedition to the Canary Islands in 40 BC and his account of the expedition was preserved by the Elder Pliny. Juba mentions Canaria, so-called for the 'multitude of dogs of great size', suggesting that these dogs were indigenous to the islands, but there is no mention of our small Bichon.

The Spaniards, on their arrival in the 15th century, also mention many large dogs, but very few other mammals: only sheep, goats and pigs. It seems likely that the Bichon was transported from the mainland by Spanish sailors, to be used for sale and barter, and for many years afterwards the Bichon remained on the islands. The late Mrs Jenkins, for many years President of the Poodle Club, recalled that on her many voyages to West Africa in the 1920s when the P&O liners called at the Canaries, the local inhabitants offered for sale to the passengers little curly-coated white dogs which Mrs Jenkins was convinced were identical to the Bichon Frisé we know today.

During the 16th century the Bichon Teneriffe became

Princess Charlotte of Wales with her pet, Lioni, *c.* 1807. Although Lioni's breed is difficult to determine, the coat looks more like that of a Bichon than a Maltese.

extremely popular in the Spanish courts. Francis José Goya y Lucientes, the Spanish painter and etcher who became court painter to Charles IV in 1789 and retained his appointment under the French occupation of Spain from 1808 to 1814, often depicted a small curly-coated lap-dog, such as the

Bichon, in his works. At roughly the same time in England Sir Joshua Reynolds, first President of the Royal Academy and the most eminent artist of his day, included a little curly-coated dog in his portraits of Miss Nelly O'Brien (in the Wallace Collection) and Miss Emilia Vansittart (now in a private collection in the USA).

The beginning of the decline of the Bichon's popularity dates from the late 19th and early 20th centuries: the little lap-dog, having been a pampered and spoiled pet, went out of fashion. It was often used in circuses and fairs, as a companion and aid to the blind, or roaming the streets, but still delighting all who crossed its path with its gay temperament and amusing ways. It is not surprising that soldiers returning from the European battle fronts of the First World War brought them home as pets. Soon afterwards, to their credit, French dog fanciers started a carefully planned breeding programme. By March 1933 the Société Centrale of France accepted a standard for the breed. This standard was drawn up by the President of the Toy Club of France, Madame Bouctovacniez, in conjuction with the Friends of the Belgian Breeds. Madam Nizet de Leemans, a breeder and international judge, subsequently suggested a more descriptive name for the breed than Bichon Teneriffe and Bichon Frisé (curly-coated lap-dog) was adopted. During 1934 the Bichon Frisé was admitted to the French Stud Book and listed by the FCI as a French/Belgian breed. Even so, the Bichon Frisé's popularity did not really increase until after the Second World War, although breeding kennels were still scarce. It is only since the breed's popularity and promotion in the USA that the Bichon on the Continent has become more in demand and therefore more have been bred.

2 The Breed Today

THE MILTON BICHONS FRISÉS

Although it has been extremely difficult to trace the history of the Continental Bichon Frisé, the breed was first officially recognised in Belgium in 1933. It appears that M and Mme Bellotte, owners of the 'Milton' prefix, were one, if not the, pioneers of the breed. Their first registered Bichon Frisé, 'Pitou', was born in 1929, this dog together with three bitches, Dora of Milton born 1933, Nanette of Milton born 1930 and Mirza, date of birth unknown, are as far back in the breed as I have been able to trace. However it is worth

Lyne of Milton, descendant of the famous Milton Bichons Frisés from the kennels of M and Mme Bellotte who did so much to establish the breed.

bearing in mind that because these four Bichons all carried
LOSH (Livre Originés St Hubert) numbers which are given
under strict surveillance by the Kennel Club of Belgium to
dogs whose pedigree is guaranteed to be pure bred for four
generations, the Milton line must go back to at least 1925.

As can be seen from the following tables the Milton lines
were very closely inbred. The history of Giselle of Milton, in
particular, is quite remarkable. Giselle, herself the result of a
father to daughter mating, appears to have been mated to all
her brothers, her sons and grandsons, and they in their turn
were equally inbred to their sons and daughters, brothers
and sisters, grandsons and granddaughters.

The tables list all the Milton dogs whose breeding I have
been able to ascertain. When using them to write out a
pedigree of, for example, Ugo de Villa Sainval, you will see
he is listed under both Int Ch Racha de Villa Sainval, his sire,
and Soraya de Villa Sainval, his dam. When a name appears
in only one table, the other parent comes from another line
or an unknown source, eg Int Ch If de la Buthiere of
Antarctica sired by Fr Ch U Sam de Villa Sainval is of pure
Milton bloodlines on one side only.

ALSH (Annexe Livre St Hubert) denotes dogs with one or
more ancestors unknown in a four-generation pedigree.

MILTON SIRES and DAMS with their progeny followed by
date of birth where known   B=bitch D=dog

Sire		Dam	
1 **Pitou 1929**		1 **Dora 1930**	
Bel Ch Bomba of Milton	B 1933	Bel Ch Pitou of Milton	D 1931
Bel Ch Pitou of Milton	D 1931		
		2 **Mirza of Milton**	
2 **Ch Pitou of Milton 1931**		Quinette of Milton	B 1942
Bambin of Milton	D 1939		
Quinette of Milton	B 1942	3 **Nanette of Milton**	
		Bel Ch Bomba of Milton	1933
3 **Bambin of Milton 1939**			
Bel Ch Ufolette of Milton	B 1946	4 **Ch Bomba of Milton 1933**	
Y-Djina of Milton	B 1948	Bambin of Milton	1939
Bel Ch Youbi of Milton	D 1949	5 **Quinette of Milton 1942**	
Zoee of Milton	B 1949	Bel Ch Ufolette of Milton	B 1946

4 Ch Youbi of Milton 1949

Abelli of Milton	D	1951
Giselle of Milton	B	1957
Hamirette of Milton	B	1958
Hanette of Milton	B	1958
Helly of Milton	B	1958
Isico of Milton	D	1959
Ivette of Milton	B	1959

5 Abelli of Milton 1951

Hodette of Milton	B	1958
Kito of Milton	D	1961

6 Helly of Milton 1958

Kwiki of Milton	D	1961
Lassy of Milton	B	1962
Lyne of Milton	B	1962

7 Isico of Milton 1959

Quillan of Milton	D	1967

8 Kito of Milton 1961

Laurette of Milton	B	1962
Lordjim of Milton	D	1962
Marouf of Milton	D	1963
Marquis of Milton	D	1963
Mowglia of Milton	D	1963
Quatna of Milton	B	1967
Quincey of Milton	B	1967
Qwiky of Milton	D	1967

9 Kwiki of Milton 1961

Maya of Milton	B	1963
Int Ch Racha de Villa Sainval	D	1968
Raya de Villa Sainval	B	1968

10 Marouf of Milton 1963

Teneriffa de la Persaliere	B	1970

11 Quillan of Milton 1967

Sandra de Villa Sainval ALSH	B	1969
Sapajou de Villa Sainval ALSH	B	1969
Sarah ALSH	B	1969
Dual Int Ch Tarzan de la Persaliere	D	1970

6 Ch Ufolette of Milton 1946

Y-Djina of Milton	B	1948
Bel Ch Youbi of Milton	B	1949
Zoee of Milton	B	1949
Abelli of Milton	D	1951
Giselle of Milton	B	1957

7 Zoee of Milton 1949

Hanette of Milton	B	1958

8 Giselle of Milton 1957

Hamirette of Milton	B	1958
Hodette of Milton	B	1958
Isico of Milton	D	1959
Ivette of Milton	B	1959
Kito of Milton	D	1961
Kwiki of Milton	D	1961
Marouf of Milton	D	1963
Marquis of Milton	D	1963
Maya of Milton	B	1963
Mowglia of Milton	B	1963
Quatna of Milton	B	1967
Qwiky of Milton	D	1967

9 Hanette of Milton 1958

Lassy of Milton	B	1962
Lyne of Milton	B	1962

10 Ivette of Milton 1959

Laurette of Milton	B	1962
Lordjim of Milton	D	1962

11 Mowglia of Milton 1963

Int Ch Racha de Villa Sainval	D	1968
Raya de Villa Sainval	B	1968
Sofia de Villa Sainval	B	1969
Soraya de Villa Sainval	B	1969
Sylvana de Villa Sainval	B	1969
Silvia de Villa Sainval	B	1969
Satan de Villa Sainval	D	1969

12 Maya of Milton 1963

Quillan of Milton	D	1967
Dual Int Ch Tarzan de la Persaliere	D	1970

Rebecca de Villa Sainval
   ALSH   B 1971
V Moustique de Villa Sainval B 1972

12 Qwiky of Milton 1967
Toscane de Villa Sainval
   ALSH   B 1970

13 Int Ch Racha de Villa Sainval 1968
Fr Ch U Sam de Villa Sainval D 1971
Ugo de Villa Sainval   D 1971
U Sacha de Villa Sainval
   ALSH   D 1971
Ullah de Villa Sainval   B 1971
Uriel de Villa Sainval   B 1971

14 Sapajou de Villa Sainval 1969
Veronique de Villa Sainval
   ALSH   B 1972
Xcarlet de Villa Sainval   B 1973
Xophie de Villa Sainval   B 1973

15 Rijou ALSH
U Trotsky ALSH   D 1971

16 Ugo de Villa Sainval 1971
Int Ch Xorba de Chaponay D 1973
Xirco de Villa Sainval   D 1973

17 U Trotsky ALSH 1971
Xandra de Chaponay   B 1973
Zarah de Chaponay   B 1975
Yvette de Chaponay   B 1974

18 U Sacha de Villa Sainval ALSH 1971
Vim de Villa Sainval ALSH   D 1972
Xcarlet de Villa Sainval   B 1973

19 Fr Ch U Sam de Villa Sainval 1971
Int Ch If de la Buthiere of
   Antarctica   D 1973
Leilah de la Buthiere
   Leijazulip   B 1975

13 Quatna of Milton 1967
Int Ch Xorba de Chaponay   D 1973
Zarah de Chaponay   B 1975

14 Quincey of Milton 1967
Sarah ALSH   B 1969
Teneriffa de la Persaliere   B 1970

15 Raya de Villa Sainval 1968
Sapajou de Villa Sainval   1969
Snow White de Villa Sainval   1969
Xophie de Villa Sainval   1973

16 Ominouche ALSH
Suzy de Villa Sainval ALSH

17 Ipoupee ALSH
Sandra de Villa Sainval ALSH B 1969

18 Soraya de Villa Sainval 1969
Fr Ch U Sam de Villa Sainval D 1971
Ugo de Villa Sainval   D 1971
Uriel de Villa Sainval   B 1971

19 Sofia de Villa Sainval 1969
Ulla de Villa Sainval   B 1971
Yalta de Villa Sainval   B 1974

20 Sandra de Villa Sainval ALSH 1969
U Sacha de Villa Sainval
   ALSH   D 1971

21 Puce ALSH
Rebecca de Villa Sainval ALSH 1971

22 Suzy de Villa Sainval ALSH
U Trotsky ALSH   D 1971

23 Toscane de Villa Sainval ALSH 1970
Veronique de Villa Sainval
   ALSH   B 1972
Vim de Villa Sainval ALSH   D 1972

24 Uriel de Villa Sainval 1971
Xcarlet de Villa Sainval   B 1973

20 **Vim de Villa Sainval ALSH** 1972
Yalta de Villa Sainval   B 1974

21 **Int Ch Xorba de Chaponay** 1973
Zethus de Chaponay of
　Tresilva   D 1975
Astor de Villa Sainval of
　Littlecourt   D 1976
Huntglen Astrid de Chaponay B 1976
Astir de Chaponay of Twinley
　　　　　　　　　　　　　　　　 D 1976
Amber de Chaponay of
　Twinley   B 1976

22 **Int Ch If de la Buthiere of
Antarctica** 1973
Eng Ch Montravia Persan
　Make Mine Mink   D 1979

23 **Zethus de Chaponay of
Tresilva** 1975
Tresilva Aura   B 1976
Eng Ch Gosmore Tresilva
　Zorba   D 1977

24 **Eng Ch Montravia Persan Make
Mine Mink** 1979
Eng & Ir Ch Tiopepi Mad
　Louie at Pamplona   D 1982

25 **Eng & Ir Ch Tiopepi Mad Louie
at Pamplona** 1982
Eng & Am Ch Sibon Sloane
　Ranger at Pamplona   D 1986

25 **Rebecca de Villa Sainval
ALSH** 1971
Toscane de Villa Sainval
　ALSH   B 1970

26 **Ullah de Villa Sainval** 1971
V Moustique de Villa
　Sainval   B 1972

27 **Veronique de Villa Sainval
ALSH** 1972
Xandra de Villa Sainval   B 1973
Yvette de Chaponay   · B 1974
Zethus de Chaponay of
　Tresilva   1975

28 **Xophie de Villa Sainval** 1973
Yalta de Villa Sainval   B 1974

29 **Xcarlet de Villa Sainval** 1973
Astir de Chaponay of
　Twinley   D 1976
Amber de Chaponay of
　Twinley   B 1976

30 **Yalta de Villa Sainval** 1974
Astor de Villa Sainval of
　Littlecourt   D 1976

31 **Yvette de Chaponay** 1974
Huntglen Astrid de Chaponay B 1976

32 **Tresilva Aura** 1976
Eng Ch Gosmore Tresilva
　Zorba   D 1977

*Extended male lines of five Bichons Frisés showing their
common Milton ancestry*

1. Bel Ch Pitou of Milton 1931
   Bambin of Milton
    Bel Ch Youbi of Milton
     Helly of Milton
      Kwiki of Milton
       Int Ch Racha de Villa Sainval
        Ugo de Villa Sainval
         Int Ch Xorba de Chaponay
          Zethus de Chaponay of Tresilva
           Ch Gosmore Tresilva Zorba

2. Bel Ch Pitou of Milton 1931
   Bambin of Milton
    Bel Ch Youbi of Milton
     Helly of Milton
      Kwiki of Milton
       Int Ch Racha de Villa Sainval
        Fr Ch U Sam de Villa Sainval
         Int Ch If de la Buthiere of Antarctica
          Aus Ch Jazz de la Buthiere of Leijazulip

3. Joy of Milton
    Fr Ch Lucky de Mortessard
     Uistiti
      Amy de Merleroux
       Int Ch Bandit de Steren Vor
        Int Ch Canard Bleu de Steren Vor
         Int Ch Gift de Steren Vor
          Int Ch Jimbo de Steren Vor
           Quintal de Wanarbry
            Peppe de Barnette
             Am Ch C & Ds Count Kristopher
              Am Ch C & Ds Beau Monde Blizzard
               Leander Beau Monde Snow Puff
                Ch Ligray Mr Beau Geste

4. Joy of Milton
    Fr Ch Lucky de Mortessard
        Uistiti
        Amy de Merleroux
            Int Ch Bandit de Steren Vor
            Eddy White de Steren Vor
                King of Rayita
                Lochinvar du Pic Four
                    Rank's Esprit du Lejerdell
                    Lejerdell's Polar Bear
                        Lejerdell's Cub de Bear
                            Cluneen Lejerdell's Silver Starshine
                            Eng Ch Cluneen Jolly Jason of
                            Hunkidori

5. Joy of Milton
    Fr Ch Lucky de Mortessard
        Uistiti
        Amy de Merleroux
            Int Ch Bandit de Steren Vor
            Eddy White de Steren Vor
                Galant de Hoop
                Jou Jou de Hoop
                    Andre de Gascoigne
                    Mex Ch Dapper Dan de Gascoigne
                        Am Ch Cali-Col's Robespierre
                        Am Ch Chaminade Mr Beau Monde
                            Am Ch Vogelflight's Choir Boy of
                            Leander

After 1969 Bichons of pure Milton breeding became obscured but research shows that progeny from Quillan of Milton ex Mowglia of Milton, Kwiki of Milton ex Mowglia of Milton, all carried the Villa Sainval prefix, Kwiki of Milton ex Mireilie of Milton carried the de la Persaliere prefix. Thus the Milton breeding continued to produce winners, including Dual Int Ch Tarzan de la Persaliere, sired by Quillan of Milton, mated to his mother Maya of Milton.

Other Bichons Frisés of note from these close-bred lines were Am Ch Little Snow White de Villa Sainval, and Int Ch Racha de Villa Sainval born 1968. Racha is an ancestor of several well-known dogs including Int Ch If de la Buthiere of Antarctica, Zethus de Chaponay of Tresilva, Am Ch Vadim de Villa Sainval, Int Ch Vania de Villa Sainval, Leilah de la Buthiere of Leijazulip, Astor de Villa Sainval of Littlecourt, and through these lines Racha is in the pedigree of many English champions.

USA

An article written by Mrs Gertrude Fournier of the famous Cali-Col Kennels provides my information on the beginning of the Bichon Frisé's history in the USA.

In 1956 a Mr and Mrs Picault emigrated to the USA from France, taking with them their four Bichons Frisés. Eddy White de Steren Vor, born 1955 (Int Ch Bandit de Steren Vor ex Amie du Lary), was a very small dog, long in body, close to the ground, with a profuse coat, silky to the touch with a dense undercoat, dark round but not bulging eyes and had a fabulous disposition, his movement left a lot to be desired and he had a very narrow chest and a distinct slope to the rump. Etoile de Steren Vor, born 1955 (Int Ch Bandit de Steren Vor ex Criquette de Steren Vor), was slightly larger with a long body and profuse coat, low to the ground, with an excellent temperament, her front and rear were not good but she had dark eyes and excellent pigmentation. Gigi de Hoop, born 1957 (Eddy White de Steren Vor ex Etoile de Steren Vor), was very large with much substance, a profuse all white coat and an excellent temperament; she was capable of having 18 and 36 cm (7 and 14 in) puppies in the same litter. Gipsie de Wanarbry, born 1957 (Int Ch Bandit de Steren Vor ex Cybele de Steren Vor), had a slightly harsher coat, pronounced colour on ear and body, dark eyes, beautiful haloes, excellent in front and rear, and movement that could not be faulted, also more compact, a fabulous temperament and the most dominant in the breed.

These Bichons Frisés, together with another import, Gavotte de Hoop, were the foundation of the breed in the USA. In May 1962 Mrs Fournier imported two bitches from Belgium, Lyne and Lassy of Milton and, later, Marquis of Milton. Lyne of Milton 7 March 1962 (Helly of Milton ex Hanette of Milton), had a short body, small, short nose, fiddle front, good rear, beautiful coat, large round black eyes and gentle ways. Lassy of Milton, Lyne's litter sister, was large, long in back, long muzzle, good front, good rear, beautiful coat and large light eyes, but was rather shy. Marquis of Milton, 7 March 1962 (Kito of Milton ex Giselle of Milton), was so ugly that he was given away as a pet without the new owners knowing he was a Bichon Frisé.

Mrs Azalea Gascoigne bought her first Bichon Frisé, Hermine de Hoop, from the Picaults in 1958. A daughter of Eddy and Etoile, she was bred to Jou Jou de Hoop, producing Avril and André de Gascoigne. While visiting France in 1962 Mrs Gascoigne attended the Paris Dog Show, buying three bitches from Madame Miligari, including Lady des Frimoussettes. Lady, when mated to André, produced the justly famous Mex Ch Dapper Dan de Gascoigne. Dapper Dan, mated to Mrs Fournier's Belgian import, Lyne of Milton, produced Am Ch Cali-Col's Candida, Ch Cali-Col's Octavius Caesar, Cali-Col's Robespierre and numerous others. Later, when Dapper Dan was mated to Cali-Col's Our Daphne, a bitch from an Eddy White and Gipsie de Wanarbry mating, they produced Am Ch Cali-Col's Scalawag, Am Ch Cali-Col's Shadrack, Am Ch Cali-Col's Winston de Noel. In all the Cali-Col Kennels bred or owned 36 American Champions. Dapper Dan, bred by Mrs Gascoigne and owned and exhibited by Mrs Myree Butler, was acknowledged as the supreme stud dog, whose name appears in the pedigree behind most top winning Bichons Frisés in the USA.

The Bichon Frisé Club of America was formed in the early 1960s. The founder, Azalea Gascoigne, became the first President, with Gertrude Fournier as Registrar and Secretary and members, Myree Butler (Reenroy), Goldie

Above Am Ch Beaumonde the Huckster and Mr Richard Beauchamp. Huckster's excellent reach and drive appear in many of his offspring, 35 of whom are already champions.

Opposite top Am Ch Chaminade Mr Beau Monde. Born in 1970, his record of siring 59 champions remains unbeaten.

Opposite below Am Ch Beaumonde the Bookie. Like Huckster (*above*), his breeders and owners are Mr Richard Beauchamp and Mrs P Waterman.

Olsen (Goldysdale), Jean Rank (Rank's) and Barbara Stubbs (Chaminade).

The breed was granted admittance by the American Kennel Club (AKC) to the Miscellaneous Classes in September 1971 and in 1972 Ch Chaminade Mr Beau Monde, bred by Mrs Stubbs and owned by Mr Richard Beauchamp, won the largest Miscellaneous Class ever held under AKC rules at the International Kennel Club of Chicago. He became and remains the top winning sire in the USA, having produced 59 champions. Born in 1970 he lived until 1984.

	Ch Cali-Col's Robespierre	Mex Ch Dapper Dan de Gascoigne
Am Ch Chaminade Mr Beau Monde		Lyne of Milton
	Ch Reenroy's Ami du Kilkanny	Mex Ch Dapper Dan de Gascoigne
		Little Nell of Cali-Col

The breed was finally admitted to regular point competition at AKS shows in April 1973.

The great upsurge in the popularity of the Bichon Frisé in the USA has been largely due to the method of presentation devised by Mrs Bernice Richardson. In 1965, in marked contrast to the usual way of showing the dogs with coats of all lengths, curly, straight, groomed or ungroomed, Mrs Richardson devised a way of scissoring the Bichon Frisé to give a neat powder-puff appearance, with the coat above the eyes cleared to show the breed's beautiful dark eyes. As a result, from being rather shaggy, untidy dogs, not unlike pet Poodles, Bichons Frisés became the lovely well-presented dogs we know today.

Milton Progeny in the USA

LYNE OF MILTON B born 1962 LOSH 207117 (Helly of Milton ex Hanette of Milton)
Am Ch Stardom's Odin Rex
Am Ch Cali-Col Candida

Am Ch Cali-Col Octavius Caesar
Cali-Col Ondine
Cali-Col Only Sam of Reenroy
Am Ch Cali-Col Robespierre
Mynette of Cali-Col
Nicol (Nichol)
Nina
Parfait Chien Sucre
Rank Gaye
Oscar of Cali-Col

LASSY OF MILTON B born 1962 LOSH 207114 (Helly of
Milton ex Hanette of Milton)
Cali-Col Pretty Penny of Reenroy
Cali-Col Prince Charming
Natchen of Cali-Col
Nelly of Cali-Col
Newsette of Cali-Col
No No Nanette of Reenroy
Nuisance

MAROUF OF MILTON D born 1963 LOSH 214632 (Kito of
Milton ex Giselle of Milton)
Tequila de la Persaliere
Tendress de la Persaliere
Teneriffa de la Persaliere
Teide de la Persaliere
Thierry de la Persaliere

MARQUIS OF MILTON born 1963 LOSH 214663 (Kito of
Milton ex Giselle of Milton)
Cali-Col Nugget
Nichol

CANADA
The first Bichons Frisés in Canada came from the American
kennels of Mrs Goldy Olson of Woodville, Washington. The
late Mrs Kay Calderbank bought her first Bichon Frisé in

		Kord Du Pic Four	**Eddy White De Steren Vor**
			Etoile De Steren Vor
	Monsieur Mieux Do Pic Four	**Kocenne De Hoop**	**Eddy White De Steren Vor**
			Ja Ja De Hoop
Petit Galant St George		**Marquis of Milton**	**Kito of Milton**
			Giselle of Milton
	Cali-Col's Nugget	**Gi Gi De Hoop**	**Eddy White De Steren Vor**
			Etoile De Steren Vor
		Andre De Gascoigne	**Jou Jou De Hoop**
			Hermine
	Mex Ch Dapper Dan De Gascoigne	**Lady Des Frimoussettes**	**Amigo Mio D'Egriselles**
			Houpette Des Frimoussettes
Ee's R Cali-Col's Ritzy Ruffles		**Eddy White De Steren Vor**	**Int Ch Bandit De Steren Vor**
			Amie Du Lary
	Cali-Col's Our Daphne	**Gipsie De Wanarbry**	**Int Ch Bandit De Steren Vor**
			Cybele De Steren Vor

Am Can Ch Ee's R Regal Prince of Henruf

One of the top winning Bichons Frisés in Canada in 1986. On the right is Mr Harry Spira, the well-known vet and judge from Australia.

1967, a bitch called Quentelly of Goldysdale, sired by Ombre de la Roche Posay ex Oree de la Roche Posay, all French breeding. Quentelly measured 9¼ in and weighed 13 lb when mature, all white with good pigment but a light eye. Mrs Calderbank then imported a dog, Vintage Year's Sautern, and a bitch, Vintage Year's Sylvaner, from Mrs H Kaiserman.

As the first breeder of Bichons Frisés in Canada Mrs Calderbank was largely responsible for the breed's recognition by the Canadian Kennel Club. Am and Can Ch EE's R Regal Prince of Henruf became the breed's first Canadian Champion, with many Best of Breed and several Group wins.

Mrs Calderbank's home-bred Can Am and Bda Ch Myworth's Enchantment owned by Dr and Mrs E Kasper became the top winning Canadian Bichon Frisé with 12 Best in Show awards. Another Canadian breeder of note is Mrs Hilda Murphy whose 'Vale Park' prefix is found in many Canadian pedigrees. For nearly eight years she published a quarterly magazine for the Bichon Frisé breeders of Canada, giving knowledge and help to the breed in its early days there.

UK

The history of the Bichon Frisé in the UK is still of relatively short duration. Although a Bichon, Espor du Kloziers owned by Mr and Mrs Hobart, was registered at the Kennel Club in 1957, it was purely a pet registration, the dog being unknown and unheard of except in Kennel Club records. Nevertheless this registration made it possible for the breed to be registered immediately on its arrival in 1974.

The first Bichon Frisé to be seen in the British showring was Cluneen Lejerdell Tarz Anna (born 3 June 1973), bred in the USA by J and D Podell, sire Int Ch Tarzan de la Persaliere, dam Teneriffa de la Persaliere, both pure Milton breeding. At the Leeds Championship Show in May 1974, judged by the late Fred Curnow, Tarz Anna won Best Non Classified, also winning first prizes at the West of England Ladies Kennel Society, Bath and Birmingham.

According to Kennel Club records Tarz Anna produced only one litter, in May 1977, three bitches and one dog, Eng Ch Cluneen Jolly Jason of Hunkidori.

During 1973 Mr and Mrs Sorstein from the USA came to live in Britain bringing with them two Bichons Frisés. The dog was Rava's Regal Valor of Reenroy born 6 February 1973, by Stardom's Odin Rex Jr ex Reenroy's Tina Tilton, bred by Stella Raabe and Myree Butler. The bitch was Jenny-Vive de Carlise, by Beaushaun's High Cotton ex Snowbee de Beaushaun bred by Mr J Bradford. These two Bichons Frisés were mated at the beginning of 1974 and this litter, born on 3 March 1974, produced five puppies: Carlise Agatha Lindee, Carlise Belinda Bear, Carlise Snowdown Star, Carlise Circe and Carlise Cicero. This was the first litter of Bichons Frisés to be registered at the Kennel Club, and was therefore the first British-bred Bichon Frisé litter. Three puppies returned to the USA, while Carlise Circe of Tresilva and Aus Ch Carlise Cicero of Tresilva became the first two British-born Bichon Frisé puppies to be exhibited in Britain. Shown first at the Brent Open Show in September 1974, Cicero won a Reserve in AVNSC with the late Eve Bentinck judging. At the Hammersmith Open Show the following month, judged by Mr W. R. Irving, Cicero won 1st Rare Breeds Puppy, 1st AV Rare Breeds Novice, Best Rare Breeds, 1st AV Minor Puppy Dog, Best Minor Puppy in Show and Reserve Best in Show. Mr Irving's critique read:

> I very much admired this youngster which moved out so well and with such smoothness and drive, good broad and slightly rounded skull, correct body proportions with the typical "overbuilt tendency" which is required of this breed. I was well aware that there would be those who would ask afterwards what I knew about this breed which is so rare in the UK, but having seen quite a large number of them in the USA felt confident that this was a good specimen and fitted well into the breed standard.

Two weeks later, on 23 October 1974, at the South-Eastern Counties Toy Dog Society Open Show, Secretary Arthur Brown scheduled for the very first time in Britain a class for Bichons Frisés with the late Ben Johnson judging. On this historic occasion Cicero won Best of Breed and Best Puppy in Show.

Aus Ch Carlise Cicero of Tresilva, one of the first Bichons Frisés to be exhibited in the UK. In October 1974, at the first show to include a class for the breed, he was Best in Breed and Best Puppy in Show.

From the very first Bichons Frisés made a great impact, gaining friends and admirers in large numbers, and when exhibited at both Open and Championship Shows were invariably in the Cards.

In March 1975 Mrs Sorstein's Bichons Frisés produced another litter, this time three bitches and two dogs. Carlise Canny Caprice became the foundation bitch of the famous 'Beaupres' Pekingese Kennels of the late Mrs E. Mirylees, Carlise Columbine the foundation bitch of Mrs Coley's Glenfolly Kennels, and Carlise Calypso Orion the foundation bitch at Mrs Vera Goold's Sidewater Kennels, owned in partnership with Mr D. Chiverton. Calypso carried the joint prefix of Mrs V. Goold and Mr D. Chiverton 'Leijazulip'.

Two other litters were born in 1975: Aus Ch Carlise Cicero of Tresilva and Carlise Circe of Tresilva produced one dog and two bitches, Le Beau Tresilva bought by Mrs E. Bothwell of Scotland, Katrinka of Carlise of Twinley bought by Mrs. P. Block, and my Bianca of Tresilva, which became the first Bichon Frisé to win a first at Crufts, and the first to win a Toy Group. The other litter, by Cluneen Jacelot de Wanarbry out of Jonquille de Wanarbry, produced five dogs on 24 June 1975.

An ancestor of today's Bichon Frisé? The 18th-century Meissen dog, modelled by J. J. Kändler, has the curly, heavily marked coat characteristic of Continental Bichons early this century. Many puppies still have pale patches on their coats.

A champion of the breed, 1985: Ch Pengorse Felicity of Tresilva, Leijazulip Gioberti ex Tresilva Marianne.

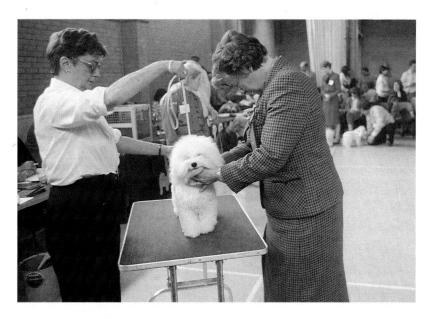

Above Ferelith Somerfield, international judge and editor-in-chief of *Dog World*, judging one of the author's dogs. Notice how she is using her hands to feel the dog's body beneath its beautifully trimmed coat.

Below Judging over and presentations made, the winners pose for the final photographs.

Right Exploring the garden—a 7-week-old Tresilva puppy.

House-training a puppy requires patience and plenty of newspaper. But Bichons Frisés are intelligent and usually learn quickly.

The next lesson is lead-training. Keep the lessons short and never drag a reluctant puppy. If it starts to pull just drop the lead, wait a few minutes and then start again.

Other imported Bichons Frisés which left quarantine in 1975 were Zethus de Chaponay of Tresilva and Zena de Chaponay of Tresilva both born 1975 and imported by myself; Aus Ch Jazz de la Buthiere of Leijazulip born 1974, and Leilah de la Buthiere of Leijazulip born 1975 by Mrs V. Goold and Mr D. Chiverton; Cluneen Jacinthe de Wanarbry, Cluneen Jessie de Wanarbry and Cluneen Joliette de Wanarbry all born in 1974 and owned by Mrs Banks; Am Ch Beau Monde the Snowdrift of Leander, born 1975, imported by Mrs W. Streatfield.

During 1975 two bitches were imported after being mated in the USA: Cottonmops Jolie Ivette of Twinley (Dominque of Quemby Du G. W. ex Petites Bon Bon De Merleoui) born 10 February 1969 imported by Mrs P. Block and Am Ch C & D's Beaumonde the Sunflower of Leander (Am Ch Chaminade Mr Beaumonde ex Am Ch C & D's Countess Becky) born 11 January 1973, imported by Mrs W. Streatfield. Both had their litters while in quarantine. On 9 September Sunflower produced four puppies, three dogs and a bitch (sired

Zethus de Chaponay of Tresilva was one of the first Bichons Frisés imported into the UK.

by Am Ch Beaumonde the Blizzard) and on 12 September
Jolie gave birth to six puppies, two bitches and four dogs,
which had been sired by Am Ch Cali-Col's Octavius Caesar.

From the first litter Leander Beaumonde Snow Puff was
bought by Mrs Chris Coley of the Glenfolly Kennels, Snow
Puff was eventually transferred during 1978 into partnership
with Mrs Coley and Mrs L. Fellowes. Snow Puff remained in
this partnership until purchased by Mrs Jean Fyfe from New
Zealand who campaigned him to his New Zealand title.
Leander Arden, bought by Mrs M. Harper of Huntglen affix,
went to Australia, while Mrs Streatfield kept Leander Snow
Carol, a bitch, and Leander Snow Venture. Of the six puppies
from Jolie, Twinley Josie Posie was bought by Mr G. Newell,
Twinley Chou Chou and Twinley Tiberius, one of the dogs,
were kept by Mrs Block for her breeding programme,
Twinley Claudius went to Mr T. Mather, and the other two
dogs were sold as pets. Later imports included:

from *Belgium*
Astor de Villa Sainval of Littlecourt 1976–1987
Amber de Chaponay of Twinley
Huntglen Astrid de Chaponay
Astir de Chaponay of Twinley
Huntglen Zara de Chaponay

from *USA*
Beau Monde the Dove of Leander
Am Ch Vogelflight's Choir Boy of Leander
C & D's Milk Punch of Leander
C & D's Little Sno White
Cali-Col's Charisma
C & D's Glory Star
Beau Monde the Ripple of Leander
Beau Monde the Spirit of Leander
Am Ch C & D's Star Maker of Leander 1975–1989
C & D's Cup of Tea of Caywood
Am Ch C & D's Prince Charles of Caywood.

from *France*
Int Ch If de la Buthiere of Antarctica 1973–1986
Noe and Nolie des Closmyons of Antarctica
Rock de la Lande Belleville
Ninon de la Buthiere of Leijazulip

From these original Bichons Frisés Aus Ch Carlise Cicero of Tresilva, Am Ch Beau Monde the Snowdrift of Leander, Aus Int & Fr Ch Jazz de la Buthiere of Leijazulip, Cali-Col's Charisma, Am Ch Beau Monde the Sunflower of Leander, Huntglen Leander Arden, Astir de Chaponay of Twinley, and Beau Monde the Dove of Leander all went to Australia.

The impact these early Bichons Frisés made is largely responsible for the breed's popularity today. The breed registrations at the Kennel Club have risen more rapidly than for any other rare breed in the UK. In 1976 31 Bichon Frisé puppies were registered, by 1988 the yearly registration had risen to 1,021.

Export of Bichons Frisés from the UK

The list of exports from this country makes interesting reading. France (with Belgium) the 'Country of Origin' of the Bichon Frisé and the USA, where the breed has been known far longer than in the UK, are the two main importers, the other top importers, Australia, Norway and Sweden, are countries where the breed was unknown until 1976.

Number of exports to:

Australia	69	New Zealand	17	S Africa	11
USA	61	Italy	15	Denmark	9
France	54	Finland	14	Canada	4
Sweden	41	Netherlands	13	Hong Kong	4
Norway	34	W Germany	12	Austria	3

Other countries that imported one or two include: Malaysia, Singapore, Japan, India, Greece, Brazil, Argentina, Portugal and Spain with several other Continental countries.

CONTINENTAL BICHONS FRISÉS

The population of Bichons Frisés in Belgium and France is still fairly small. As the FCI forbid the scissoring of coats Continental breeders have, until very recently, presented their long-haired dogs in a fairly natural condition, Bichon Frisé breeders being no exception. Without presentation the breed's main beauty is hidden: it is very difficult to appreciate the lovely head, black eyes and nose when covered in an untidy coat or when the dog is ungroomed. The breed's popularity was greatly enhanced in the USA by superb presentation and with its increasing popularity in the UK, Continental breeders are very slowly beginning to present their dogs in a more glamorous way.

It has been difficult to trace the pedigrees and lines of the French Bichons Frisés. Fr Ch Lucky de Mortessard, one of the earliest dogs registered in France (Livre des Originés, Number LOF 20), was sired by Joy of Milton, a Belgian dog. Most Bichons in old pedigrees, such as Uisiti, Amy de Merleroux, Int Ch Bandit de Steren Vor, Int Ch Canard Bleu, and the well-known Am Ch C & D's Count Kristopher, to name a few, are all descendants on the male side of this French champion Lucky.

The late Madame Laisne on visiting Teneriffe brought back two Bichons of unknown parentage, a dog Kamin and a bitch Lilith, the descendants of these two Bichons are behind most of the Closmyons, including Int Ch Quetty des Closmyons.

When studying the pedigrees of the many champions bred by Madame Desfarges' la Buthiere Bichons, two Belgian Bichons frequently occur: Fr Ch U Sam de Villa Sainval and Fr Ch Vania de Villa Sainval, both come from pure Milton lines. In fact Milton lines occur in most Continental pedigrees.

During the past 14 years 54 British Bichons Frisés were exported to France and recorded in the Kennel Club Stud Book Breed Records, and therefore were sold with an export pedigree. Others without this pedigree are impossible to trace, but sources in France tell me there are a lot of British-bred Bichons Frisés in the Paris area. A few have also gone to Germany, Italy and the Netherlands, so British Bichons Frisés are helping to increase the Continental population.

Affixes of Continental breeders 1925–1976

FRANCE
Bourbiel – Mlle Meynieu
la Buthiere – Mme Desfarges
Closmyons – Mme Laisne
Frimoussettes – Mme Miligari
Lande de Belleville – Mme Darolt
Roi des Lutins – Mme Naudet
Steren Vor – Mme Abadie
Wanarbry – Mme Mazeas-Nicholas

BELGIUM
Chaponay – Mme Vansteenkiste-Deleu
Milton – M & Mme Bellotte
la Persaliere – M Baras
Villa Sainval – M & Mme Baras to 1975 Mme Berben from 1976

GERMANY
Dandelion – Frau Kappels
Dierstein – Frau Neumeiller

SWEDEN
Apparently a Bichon Frisé owned by a Belgian diplomat was exhibited in Sweden in the late 1950s. Although exhibited for several years it was generally considered to be a rather odd Poodle, and from that time until 1976 the breed was completely unknown.

Int Ch Tresilva Don Azur, one of the first Bichons Frisés to be imported into Sweden, had an extremely successful show career.

The first Bichons Frisés to be seen since then were introduced by Mrs Jane Martinsson-Vesa. During 1976 Int Ch Tresilva Don Azur and Sw Ch Tresilva Donna Azur, bred by myself by Aus Ch Carlise Cicero of Tresilva ex Zena de Chaponay of Tresilva, and Am & Nordic Ch Paw Paw Rhinestone Cowboy, born 24 April 1976, bred by Mrs Amy Costello and L. Goldwater, by Am Ch Paw Paw Punjab ex Goldwater's Bellisima Biji, made their appearance in the showring. Don and Donna were shortly followed by Nor Ch Beaupres Candida of Tresilva (Zethus de Chaponay of Tresilva ex Carlise Canny Caprice of Beaupres) bred February 1977 by Mrs Betty Mirylees and Miss Fiona Mirylees.

Tresilva Don Azur became the first Bichon Frisé to win the titles of Swedish, Nordic and Int Champion Bichon Frisé of the year 1977/8, and in 1978 was third in the Toy Group Top Winners List, winning in all 15 CACIBs, 34 CCs and 34 Best of Breeds.

Am Ch Paw Paw Rhinestone Cowboy, when mated to Sw Ch Tresilva Donna Azur, sired the first Swedish Champion, Sw Ch Azur André, bred by Mrs Martinsson-Vesa and owned and exhibited by Madame F. Brunberg-Karlsson. Further imports to Sweden in 1977 were Eva Soderqvist's Nor Ch Twinley King Kassius, bred by Mrs Block, Leijazulip The Tinker (Aus Ch Beau Monde the Snowdrift of Leander ex Carlise Calypso Orion) exported by Mrs Kesper to Mr K. Davidsson and Leijazulip Dominique (Aus Ch Jazz de la Buthiere of Leijazulip ex Leilah de la Buthiere of Leijazulip) exported by D. Chiverton & Mrs V. Goold and both bred by them.

These were the first of many Bichons Frisés imported from the UK.

NORWAY

In 1977 the first Bichons Frisés imported to Norway from Britain were Leijazulip Danielle born 6 February 1977 by Aus Ch Jazz de la Buthiere of Leijazulip ex Carlise Calypso Orion and Leijazulip Philipe born 8 February 1977 by Aus Ch Jazz de la Buthiere of Leijazulip ex Leilah de la Buthiere of Leijazulip. Both were bred and exported by Mrs V. Goold and Mr D. Chiverton and owned by Mrs L. Robinson.

The first Bichon to obtain the title of Int Ch and considered to have improved the quality of the breed in Norway was Huntglen Nolie, an Int Ch If de la Buthiere of Antarctica granddaughter, imported by Mr and Mrs Haakon Strand. Nolie mated to Nor Ch Sankt Obrit Chivas produced the first Norwegian-bred Champion: Nor Ch Lollipop My Boy. Chivas, a son of Int Ch Tresilva Don Azur, owned by Brit Nielson is considered the top sire, having sired many Norwegian champions.

In addition to the Tresilva Bichons Frisés imported in 1980 from the UK, Dr B. Eskeland also imported the first American Bichons Frisés including Am Ch Primo Tugg-O-War. These American champion imports have added to the breed's improvement and progress in Norway.

AUSTRALIA

The Powder-Puff Dog, the Bichon Frisé, very quickly excited the interest of a large number of the dog fraternity when the breed was first exhibited in Australia. Mr and Mrs Mackenzie-Begg were pioneers of the breed, importing from the UK Am & Aus Ch Beau Monde the Snowdrift of Leander, a dog born 2 January 1975, bred by Mr R. Beauchamp and Jean Ellis, sired by Am Ch Chaminade Mr Beau Monde out of Am Ch Works D'Artes A Chaminade. Snowdrift went to Australia after a brief stay in the UK from mid 1975 to July 1976, during which time he sired only three litters, two under the Leander prefix and one under Leijazulip. Snowdrift caused a sensation, very quickly winning top awards whenever shown and was the first Bichon Frisé to obtain the title of Australian Champion.

Also at the end of 1976 Mrs D. Crosby-Browne imported four puppies from two litters born in the UK: Leander Snow Scout and Leander Snow Bubble born 10 May 1976 by Am Ch Beau Monde the Snowdrift of Leander ex Am Ch Beau Monde the Sunflower and Leander Snow Cap and Leander Snow Girl born 6 May by Am Ch C & D's Beau Monde the Blizzard ex Val Va Don's Demi Chantee.

Mr and Mrs Mackenzie-Begg then imported from the UK Aus & Am Ch Beau Monde the Dove of Leander bred by Mr R. Beauchamp and Pauline Waterman born 10 December 1975 by Am Ch C & D's Count Kristopher ex Am Ch Beau Monde the Vamp, and Aus Ch Carlise Cicero of Tresilva born 3 March 1974 by Rava's Regal Valor of Reenroy ex Jenny-Vive de Carlise bred by Mrs Sorstein and exported by myself.

Since the beginning of 1976 many more Bichons Frisés have been imported, both from the USA and Britain, foremost of which was Aus & Int Ch Jazz de la Buthiere of Leijazulip born 17 October 1974 by Int Ch If de la Buthiere of Antarctica ex Vanda de la Buthiere. Jazz was bought by Mrs V. Goold and Mr D. Chiverton from the la Buthiere Kennels of Madame Desfarges in 1975. After success both in

Aus Ch Jazz de la Buthiere of Leijazulip was bred in France by Mme Desfarges in 1974. Imported into the UK by Mrs Goold and Mr Chiverton, he later went to Australia where he had a successful career.

the showring and as a sire in the UK he is now owned and was exhibited by Mr Frank Vallely and Mr Rudy Van Voorst of the Azara Kennels and became the top winning Bichon Frisé in Australia.

I am indebted to Rudy Van Voorst for up-to-date news of Bichons Frisés in Australia. Undoubtedly Aus Ch Jazz de la Buthiere of Leijazulip has had the greatest influence, certainly on the Bichons Frisés in New South Wales. Having won 20 Best in Show and 50 Toy Groups, he remains the top sire with 31 champions to his credit.

Leijazulip Angelique, a Jazz daughter also imported by the Azara Kennels, is the dam of 14 champions which include Aus Ch Azara Ma Belle Ami, Aus Ch Azara Petite Fleur, Aus Ch Azara le President, and Int Ch Azara Petite Carman. Ma Belle Ami and Petite Fleur were the results of a father to daughter mating.

Another import, Eng & Aus Ch Leijazulip Jazz of Zudiki, a Jazz grandson owned by Wendy and John Hutchison, has sired 22 champions.

Of the 75 Bichons Frisés exported to Australia since 1976 most came from Britain, other Australian Champions are mainly descended from the Leander and Tresilva imports and Beau Monde dogs from the USA.

The Australian standard is the same as the British Kennel Club's standard which is based on the original FCI Standard. The Bichon is exhibited in the Toy Group.

Presentation, which is based largely on the American style (page 26), has played a large part in the acceptance of the breed in Australia. It was fortunate for the breed that the early Bichons Frisés went to owners with experience in presenting coated dogs.

By 1987 the breed registrations in Australia had reached 454.

NEW ZEALAND

Mr and Mrs Crooks introduced the breed to New Zealand early in 1977 with the first NZ Ch Beaupres Casanova born 3 February 1977 by Zethus de Chaponay of Tresilva ex Carlise Canny Caprice of Beaupres and Beaupres Astrid born 31 August 1977 by Astor de Villa Sainval of Littlecourt ex Carlise Canny Caprice of Beaupres, both bred by Mrs E. Mirylees. At the end of 1977 Mrs Ealand imported Pyrillon Coffee Truffle born 18 May 1977, bred by Mr and Mrs C. Bowker by Aus Ch Jazz de la Buthiere of Leijazulip ex Leijazulip the Snowmaiden. Mr and Mrs Crooks bred the first litter of Bichons Frisés in New Zealand during November 1978.

Mrs Jean Fyffe imported Bichons Frisés from the Azara Kennels in Australia. These, together with more recent imports from the UK, have helped to improve and establish the breed in New Zealand.

3 The Breed Standards

FEDERATION CYNOLOGIQUE
INTERNATIONALE (FCI)
STANDARD: BICHON A POIL FRISE
RACE FRANCO-BELGE

Apparence générale. Petit chien gai et enjoué, d'allure vive, à museau de longeur moyenne, à poil long tirebouchonné très lâche, ressemblant à la fourrure de la chèvre de Mongolie. Le port de tête est fier et haut, les yeux foncés sont vifs et expressifs.

Tête. Le crâne, plus long que museau, tête en harmonie comparée au corps.

Truffe. La truffe est arrondie, bien noire, à grain fin et luisant.

Lèvres. Les lèvres sont fines, assez sèches, moins toutefois que chez le schipperke, ne tombant que juste ce qu'il faut pour que la lèvre inférieure soit couverte, mais jamais lourdes ni pendantes; elles sont normalement pigmentées de noir jusqu'aux commissures; la lèvre inférieure ne peut pas être lourde ni apparente, ni molle et ne laisse pas voir les muqueuses quand la gueule est fermée.

Denture. La denture est normale, c'est-à-dire que les dents incisives de la mâchoire inférieure viennent se placer immédiatement contre et derrière la pointe des dents de la mâchoire supérieure.

Museau. Le museau ne doit pas être épais ni lourd, sans cependant être pincé; les joues sont plates et pas très musculeuses. Le stop est peu accentué, la gouttière entre les arcades sourcilières légèrement apparente.

Int Ch Quetty de Closmyons, a descendant of two Bichons bought
by Mme Laisne in Teneriffe after the last war.

Yeux. Les yeux foncés, autant que possible bordés de paupières foncées; sont de forme plutôt arrondie et non amande;
ils ne sont pas placés obliquement, sont vifs, pas trop grands,
ne laissant pas voir de blanc. Ils ne sont ni gros ni proéminents, comme ceux du griffon bruxellois et du pékinois;
l'orbite ne doit pas être saillante. Le globe de l'oeil de doit
pas ressortir de façon exagérée.
Crâne. Le crâne est plutôt plat au toucher, bien que la
garniture le fasse paraître rond.
Oreilles. Les oreilles sont tombantes, bien garnies de poils
finement frisés et longs, portées plutôt en avant quand
l'attention est éveillée, mais de façon que le bord antérieur
touche au crâne et ne s'en écarte pas obliquement; la
longueur du cartilage ne doit pas aller, comme chez le
caniche, jusqu'à la truffe, mais s'arrête à la moitié de la
longueur du museau. Elles sont, du reste, bien moins larges
et plus fines que chez ce chien.
Encolure. L'encolure est assez longue, portée haut et fière

ment. Elle est ronde et fine près du crâne, s'élargissant graduellement pour s'emboîter sans heurt dans les épaules. Sa longueur est très approximativement un tiers de la longueur du corps (proportion de 11 cm à 33 cm pour un sujet de 27 cm de haut); les pointes de l'épaule contre le garrot étant prises comme bases.

Epaule. L'épaule est assez oblique, pas proéminente, donnant l'apparence d'être de même longueur que le bras, environ 10 cm, celui-ci n'est pas écarté du corps et le coude en particulier n'est pas en dehors.

Pattes. Les pattes sont droites vues de face, bien d'aplomb, fines d'ossature; le paturon est court et droit vu de face, très légèrement oblique vu de profil. Les ongles seront de préférence noirs; c'est un idéal toutefois difficile à atteindre.

Poitrine. La poitrine est bien développée, le sternum prononcé, les fausses côtes arrondies et ne finissant pas brusquement, la poitrine ayant horizontalement une assez grande profondeur.

Flancs. Les flancs sont bien relevés au ventre, le peau y est fine et non flottante, donnant une apparence assez levrettée.

Rein. Le rein est large et bien musclé légèrement bombé. Le bassin est large, la croupe légèrement arrondie, le fouet est planté un peu plus sous la ligne du dos que chez le caniche.

Cuisses. Les cuisses sont larges et bien musclées: les rayons bien obliques, le jarret est aussi plus coudé que chez le caniche, le pied nerveux.

Queue. Normalement la queue est portée relevée et gracieusement recourbée, dans le plan de l'épine dorsale, sans être enroulée, elle n'est pas écourtée et ne peut rejoindre le dos; toutefois, la garniture du poil peut retomber sur le dos.

Pigmentation. La pigmentation sous le poil blanc est foncée de préfèrence; les organes sexuels sont alors pigmentés de teinte noire ou bleuâtre ou beige.

Couleur. Blanc pur.

Poil. Fin, soyeux, tirebouchonné très lâche, ressemblant à celui de la fourrure de la chèvre de Mongolie, ni plat, ni cordé et atteignant 7 à 10 cm.

Toilette. Le chien peut être présenté avec les pieds et le museau légèrement dégagés.

Taille. La hauteur au garrot ne doit pas dépasser 30 cm, la petite taille étant un élément de succès.

Défauts graves. Disqualifications: prognathisme (grignage— bégu) si développé que les incisives ne se touchent plus—Nez rose, lèvres couleur chair, yeux pâles, cryptorchidie, monorchidie, queue enrouleé et tourneé en hêlice. Taches noires dans le poil.

Défauts à éviter. Pigmentation se prolongeant dans le poil de façon à former taches rousses. Poil plat, ondulé, cordé ou trop court. Légèrement prognathe ou bégu.

The original standard for the Bichon Frisé

In March of 1933 the following Breed Standard was adopted by the Société Centrale in France.

General Appearance. A little dog, gay and joyful, with a medium-size muzzle and long hair curling loosely. Dark eyes are bright and expressive. Viewed from the side giving a slightly roached appearance.

Head. The cranium is larger than the nose and will measure approximately from two inches to three and one-half inches, the circumference of the cranium corresponding to the height of the withers, about ten and one-half inches. The nose is rounded, definitely black, smooth and glossy.

Lips. Fine, somewhat dry but less than the Schipperke, never drooping and heavy, they are normally pigmented black, the lower lip should not be heavy or noticeable but should not be soft and not let the mucous membrane show when the mouth is closed.

Mouth. Normal, the fore teeth of the lower jaw should be against and behind the points of the upper teeth (scissors).

Muzzle. Should not be thick and heavy but not pinched. The cheeks are flat and not muscular, the stop accentuated slightly.

Eyes. Dark, as much as possible surrounded by black, are rather round and not almond-shaped. They should not be placed at an oblique angle, are lively, not too large, not showing any white when looking forward. They should not be too big and prominent like the Pekingese. The eye socket should not sag and the eye globe should not bulge in an exaggerated manner.

Cranium. Rather flat to the touch although the fur gives a round appearance.

Ears. Drooping, well covered with long wavy hair, carried rather forward when at attention, the length of the cartilage cannot reach the truffle as the French Poodle but only halfway the length of the muzzle. In fact they are not as large and are finer than those of the Poodle.

Crest (or neck). Rather long. Carried highly and proudly, it is round and fine, close to the cranium, widening gradually to meet the withers. Its length is approximately one-third of the length of the body (proportion being about four and one-half inches to thirteen and one-half inches for a subject eleven inches high).

Withers. Are rather oblique, not prominent, giving the appearance of being as long as the forearm, approximately four inches. Forearm should not be spread out from the body and the elbow, in particular should not point outward.

Legs. Are straight when looking from the front, of good standing, of fine bones, the pastern short and straight when viewed from the front, very slightly oblique from the profile view, the toenails should be black by preference, but it is difficult to obtain.

Chest. Well-developed, the sternum is pronounced, the lower ribs rather round and not ending abruptly, the chest being horizontally rather deep. The flanks are close to the belly, the skin is fine and not floating.

Loin. Large and muscular. The hock is more elbowed than the Poodle.

Tail. Is normally carried upwards and gracefully curved over the dorsal spine, the hair of the tail is long and will lay on the back.

Pigmentation. Under the white hair skin is preferably dark. The sexual organs are also pigmented black, bluish or beige, as the spots often found on the body.

Colour. Preferably all white, sometimes white with tan or grey on the ears and body.

Hair. Should be fine, silky and loosely curled, its length being approximately two and one-half inches to four inches long. Unlike the Maltese, the Bichon Frisé also has an undercoat.

Size. The height at the withers cannot be over twelve inches, the smaller dog being the element of success.

Reason for disqualification. Over and undershot, inferior prognathism, pink nose, flesh-coloured lips, pale eyes, tail curled in a corkscrew manner, black spots in the fur.

AMERICAN KENNEL CLUB STANDARD

General Appearance. The Bichon Frisé is a small, sturdy, white powder puff of a dog whose merry temperament is evidenced by his plumed tail carried jauntily over the back and his dark eyed inquisitive expression.

Coming and going, his movement is precise and true. In profile, he measures the same from withers to ground as from withers to set of tail. The body from the forward most point of the sternum to the buttocks is slightly longer than height at the withers. He moves with steady topline and easy reach and drive.

Head. The head is covered with a topknot of hair that creates an overall rounded impression. The skull is slightly rounded allowing for a round and forward looking eye. A properly balanced head is three parts muzzle to five parts skull, measured from the nose to the slightly accentuated stop and from stop to occiput; a line drawn between the outside corners of the eyes and to the nose will create a near equilateral triangle. There is a slight degree of chiseling under the eyes, but not so much as to result in a weak or snipey foreface. The lower jaw is strong.

Nose – is prominent and always black.

Teeth – meet in a scissors bite. An undershot or overshot jaw should be severely penalized. A crooked or out of line tooth is permissible, however, missing teeth are to be severely faulted.

Eyes – are round, black or dark brown and are set in the skull to look directly forward. An overly large or bulging eye is a fault as is an almond shaped, obliquely set eye. Halos, the black or very dark brown skin surrounding the eyes, are necessary as they accentuate the eye and enhance expression. The eye rims themselves must be black. Broken pigment or total absence of pigment in the eye rims produce a blank and staring expression which is a definite fault. Yellow, blue or grey eyes are a serious fault and should be severely penalized.

Ears – are dropped and are covered with long flowing hair. When extended toward the nose, the leathers should reach approximately halfway the length of the muzzle. They are set on slightly higher than eye level and rather forward on the skull, so that when the dog is alerted they serve to frame the face.

Lips – are black, fine, never drooping.

Neck and Body.

Neck – The arched neck is long and carried proudly and gracefully behind an erect head. It blends smoothly into the shoulders. The length of neck from occiput to withers is approximately one third the distance from sternum to buttocks.

Body – The topline is level except for a slight arch over the loin.

Sternum – is well pronounced and protrudes slightly forward of the point of shoulder.

Chest – is well developed and wide enough to allow free and unrestricted forward movement of the front legs.

Ribcage – is moderately sprung and extends back to a short and muscular loin.

Tail – is well plumed, set on level with the topline and is curved gracefully over the back so that the hair of the tail rests on the back. A low tail set, a tail carried perpendicularly to the back, or a tail which droops behind should be severely penalized. When the tail is extended toward the head it should reach at least half way to the withers. A corkscrew tail is a very serious fault.

Forequarters

Shoulders – The shoulder blade, upper arm and forearm should be approximately equal in length. The shoulders are laid back to somewhat near a forty-five degree angle. The upper arm extends well back so the elbow is placed directly below the withers when viewed from the side.

Legs – should be of medium bone, not too fine or too coarse, straight with no bow or curve in the forearm or wrist. The elbows are held close to the body.

Pasterns – slope slightly from the vertical.

Feet – are tight and round resembling those of a cat and point directly forward, turning neither in nor out.

Pads – are black.

Nails – are kept short, the dewclaws may be removed.

Hindquarters – are of medium bone, well angulated with muscular thighs and spaced moderately wide. The upper and lower thigh are nearly equal in length meeting at a well bent stifle joint. The leg from hock joint to foot pad is perpendicular to the ground. Paws are tight and round with black pads. Dewclaws may be removed.

Cowhocks are a very serious fault.

Coat.

Texture – of the coat is of utmost importance. The undercoat is soft and dense, the outercoat of a coarser and curlier texture. The combination of the two gives a soft but substantial feel to the touch which is similar to plush or velvet and when patted springs back. When bathed and brushed it stands off the body, creating an overall powder puff appearance. A wirey coat is not desirable. A silky coat is a fault. A coat that lies down and lack of undercoat are very serious faults.

Trimming – The coat is trimmed to reveal the natural outline of the body. It is rounded off from any direction and never cut so short as to create an overly trimmed or squared off appearance. The furnishings of the head, beard, moustache, ears and tail are left longer. The topline should be trimmed to appear level. The coat should be long enough to maintain the powder puff look which is characteristic of the breed.

Color – is white, may have shadings of buff, cream or apricot around the ears or on the body. Any color in excess of 10% of the entire coat of a mature specimen is a fault and should be penalized, but color of the accepted shadings should not be faulted in puppies.

Gait – Movement at a trot is free, precise and effortless. In profile the forelegs and hindlegs extend equally with an easy reach and drive that maintains a steady topline. When moving, the head and neck should remain somewhat erect and as speed increases there is a very slight convergence of legs toward the center line.

Paddling or toeing in are faults.

Moving away, the hindquarters travel with moderate width between them and the foot pads can be seen.

Hocks that strike each other or are thrown out to the sides are faults.

Size – Dogs and Bitches 9½ to 11½ inches should be given primary preference. Only where the comparative superiority of a specimen outside these ranges clearly justifies it, should greater latitude be taken. In no case, however, should this latitude ever extend over 12 inches or under 9 inches. The minimum limits do not apply to puppies.

Temperament – Gentle mannered, very sensitive, playful and affectionate. A cheerful attitude is the hallmark of this breed and one should settle for nothing less.

UK KENNEL CLUB BREED STANDARD

General Appearance. Well balanced dog of smart appearance, closely coated with handsome plume carried over the back. Natural white coat curling loosely. Head carriage proud and high.

Characteristics. Gay, happy, lively little dog.

Temperament. Friendly and outgoing.

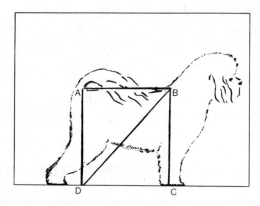

The area represented between the points A, B, C and D should give the impression of a square. The diagonal between B and D denotes the true angle of the neck and lay back of the stifle.

Correct conformation.

Incorrect conformation.

Head & Skull. Ratio of muzzle length to skull length 3:5. On a head of the correct width and length, lines drawn between the outer corners of the eyes and nose will create a near equilateral triangle. Whole head in balance with body. Muzzle not thick, heavy nor snipey. Cheeks flat, not very strongly muscled. Stop moderate but definite, hollow between eyebrows just visible. Skull slightly rounded, not coarse, with hair accentuating rounded appearance. Nose large, round, black, soft and shiny.

Eyes. Dark, round with black rims, surrounded by dark haloes, consisting of well pigmented skin. Forward-looking, fairly large but not almond shaped, neither obliquely set nor protruding. Showing no white when looking forward. Alert, full of expression.

Ears. Hanging close to head, well covered with flowing hair longer than leathers, set on slightly higher than eye level and rather forward on skull. Carried forward when dog alert, forward edge touching skull. Leather reaching approximately half-way along muzzle.

Mouth. Jaws strong, with a perfect, regular and complete scissor bite, i.e. the upper teeth closely overlapping the lower teeth and set square to the jaws. Full dentition desirable. Lips fine, fairly tight and completely black.

Neck. Arched neck fairly long, about one third length of body. Carried high and proudly. Round and slim near head, gradually broadening to fit smoothly into shoulders.

Forequarters. Shoulders oblique, not prominent, equal in length to upper arm. Upper arm fits close to body. Legs straight, perpendicular, when seen from front; not too finely boned. Pasterns short and straight viewed from front, very slightly sloping viewed from side.

Body. Forechest well developed, deep brisket. Ribs well sprung, floating ribs not terminating abruptly. Loin broad, well muscled, slightly arched and well tucked up. Pelvis broad, croup slightly rounded. Length from withers to tailset should equal height from withers to ground.

Hindquarters. Thighs broad and well rounded. Stifles well

bent; hocks well angulated and metatarsals perpendicular.
Feet. Tight, rounded and well knuckled up. Pads black. Nails preferably black.
Tail. Normally carried raised and curved gracefully over the back but not tightly curled. Never docked. Carried in line with backbone, only hair touching back; tail itself not in contact. Set on level with topline, neither too high nor too low. Corkscrew tail undesirable.
Gait/Movement. Balanced and effortless with an easy reach and drive maintaining a steady and level topline. Legs moving straight along line of travel, with hind pads showing.
Coat. Fine, silky, with soft corkscrew curls. Neither flat nor corded, and measuring 7–10cm in length. The dog may be presented untrimmed or have muzzle and feet slightly tidied up.
Colour. White, but cream or apricot markings acceptable up to 18 months. Under white coat, dark pigment desirable. Black, blue or beige markings often found on skin.
Size. Ideal height 23–28cm (9–11in) at withers.
Faults. Any departure from the foregoing points should be considered a fault and the seriousness with which the fault should be regarded should be in exact proportion to its degree.
Note. Male animals should have two apparently normal testicles fully descended into the scrotum.

NOTES ON THE BREED STANDARD
A Breed Standard is an attempt to describe the ideal dog for guidance to breeders when planning a breeding programme and for show judges who by their ability to interpret the Standard are capable of placing the dogs in the order which, in their opinion, adheres most closely to the Standard. In effect a Breed Standard is an analysis of a breed written as a word-picture for the betterment of the breed and to establish a breed type.

The Standard for the Bichon Frisé was planned and written soon after the First World War by the early breeders and was accepted by the FCI in 1933. Since that time, although slight differences of opinion occur in all countries, the Standard has remained much the same and is invariably used to protect and advance the future of the breed.

GENERAL APPEARANCE This clause is fairly straightforward. When we look at the Bichon Frisé we should be able to see if it is well balanced, neither short on leg making it appear long in back, or too long in leg and too short in back, resembling a Poodle. Good head carriage can only be achieved by a good reach of neck. A well plumed tail carried loosely over the back together with the natural white curly coat contribute to a smart appearance.

CHARACTERISTICS. The dark expressive eyes, alert attitude, and gaily carried tail demonstrate these requirements very clearly.

TEMPERAMENT. No problem here, the Standard is explicit.

HEAD AND SKULL. The head of any breed is of the greatest importance, without the correct head and expression a breed loses type. The Bichon Frisé's head must have the correct proportions as without them the head can easily resemble that of a Poodle. The Standard is very clear on the correct proportions, the original French Standard (page 43) even more so. If the zygomatic arch falls away behind the eyes the eye placement is altered, either they become small and close set or they lose the required roundness and become almond-shaped. The skull is slightly rounded. The distance between the two outer corners of each eye should measure the same as from the outer corners of the eyes to the tip of the nose, creating an equilateral triangle. The nose should be completely black.

EYES. The original French standard uses two words: 'grands' (large) and 'gros' (big, bulky or stout), the Standard calls for a large eye but not so large as to show the white of eye, nor as big or bulky as the Pekingese or Griffon. In other words the eyes should be dark, large, wide apart but not protruding.

Broken pigment on eye rims should be penalised, any lack of pigment or haloes completely spoils the Bichon Frisé's correct expression.

EARS. Many Bichons Frisés have ears set too high, therefore the forward edge does not touch the skull when the dog is alert, neither do the leathers reach halfway along the muzzle.

MOUTH. The correct dentition is a scissor bite, ie top teeth just overlapping the lower teeth. An undershot jaw with the lower teeth overlapping the top teeth is a bad fault and a dog with this characteristic should not be used for breeding.

NECK. The length of neck in the Bichon Frisé should measure a third of the body length measured from sternum to pin-bone, this length of neck allows for the good head carriage without which the overall balance and good outline is completely spoilt.

FOREQUARTERS. The shoulder-blade should meet the upper arm at an angle of 90°, with the blade well laid back and the length of the scapula equal to the length of the humerus the dog will have good reach in its forward stride. Elbows should be close to the body. Legs quite straight but with a slight slope to the pastern when viewed from the side.

BODY. Measuring the same from withers to ground as from withers to tail, the back has a slight rise over the loin. Although not mentioned in the Standard the sternum protrudes beyond the point of shoulder, this point being where the scapula joins the humerus. The distance from the point of shoulder to the pin bone measures approximately a third longer than the height at the withers.

HINDQUARTERS. Well muscled with good angulation between the pelvis and the femur. Hip bones should leave the spinal column at an angle of 30°. The stifle is well angulated. Legs parallel to each other, neither too close or too wide. Hock to heel perpendicular to ground, the hock is more pronounced than that of the Poodle. When standing naturally the Bichon Frisé's legs should not extend well behind the body, such over angulated legs will not keep up with the movement of the forequarters, thereby losing both balance and rhythm.

FEET. Tight, well cushioned like a cat's paw, the pads should be black. Black nails are desirable but difficult to obtain.

TAIL. Curved over the back set on level with the topline, the tail must not touch the back, be carried perpendicular or be tightly curled. A kink or corkscrew tail is a serious fault. It is only the long feathering that falls on the back, a tail with the correct set will always show daylight under the curve when the dog is moving. A stationary tail clamped on the back is quite wrong, as is a tail held perpendicular.

GAIT/MOVEMENT. Legs should move straight and parallel with both reach and drive, a quick shuffling movement is quite wrong. When moving away the back black pads should be clearly visible.

COAT. The soft undercoat is essential, and, with the fine silky curly topcoat, gives the soft dense coat which springs back when touched. A coarse feel to the coat is quite wrong as is a straight coat, or when lacking undercoat, the hair lies flat on the body. The coat is not as coarse as the Poodle's or as fine as the Maltese's.

COLOUR. White, pale beige or tan markings often occur on puppies and young dogs. These colours usually fade on maturity and should be completely gone by 18 months at the latest. Pigmentation is a far more important issue in this breed, because once lost in any breeding it can be extremely difficult to regain. The Bichon Frisé should have black nose, pads, eye-rims and dark pigmented skin above the eyes. The French Standard also calls for black or dark pigmentation on the sexual organs. Black, blue or beige pigment is often found on the skin. Although not previously recorded, I have noticed that the roof of the mouth of a well-pigmented Bichon Frisé is usually completely black.

JUDGING THE BICHON FRISÉ

All coated breeds are more difficult to judge than the smooth-coated ones where most of the anatomy can be seen and assessed without using one's hands. The Bichon is particularly difficult to judge because presentation is such an art—and so artful—that many facets can be scissored to give a false impression. It is therefore absolutely necessary when judging this breed that judges use their hands in order to assess whether certain important requirements in the Standard have been met.

Let us start with the head. It is easy to see the colour, size and shape of the eyes and also to see that they are set forward looking and fairly wide apart. The haloes and eye-rims can also be seen quite clearly, but everything else must be felt. Ear set, shape of the skull, width of the zygomatic arch, length of the skull from stop to occiput—all these important points are completely hidden by the thick dense coat and must be felt.

The length of neck, so often an illusion, cannot be assessed without a judge's hands. Lay-back of shoulder, length of forearm, the boning in the quarters, the bend of stifle, the spring of rib, correct topline and depth of brisket, the set of tail, tail without kink or corkscrew, or the muscular condition, none can be ascertained without using one's hands.

The overall balance of the Bichon Frisé is fairly easy to see, but even this can be improved by clever scissoring. Only by using their hands will judges find the flat zygomatic arch that means the skull is too narrow, or an upright shoulder and a short forearm from which they will know that the dog cannot move correctly in front or, if it has straight stifles or crooked hocks, that it cannot move true at the rear.

To be a good judge one should never be swayed by good and clever presentation alone, always look, or feel, for the dog under the coat.

4 The Bichon Frisé puppy

CHOOSING A PUPPY
When you are considering buying a puppy there are a few
things that should be considered carefully before you bring a
puppy into your home and family. Young puppies in their
early days require as much, if not more, care and patience as
a very young child. For the first few weeks the puppy also
will require much of your time, but time spent in early
training will be amply rewarded.

The Bichon Frisé, being small, is most suitable for the
family in a small house with a reasonable garden or for the
owner who lives in a flat but enjoys a daily walk in the park.
The Bichon Frisé is, however, a very sturdy dog so is perfectly
at home in the country, and it is by no means unknown for
them to catch the occasional rabbit.

As you were probably attracted to the breed by its lovely
white curly coat it will come as no surprise that this requires
daily grooming and unless you are able to bath, comb, brush
and cut the long coat, your Bichon Frisé will require regular
visits to the grooming parlour, which is an added expense.
However, as the coat does not shed, at least you will not find
hairs all over your furniture.

The sex of the puppy you decide to have is a matter of
personal choice, but in my opinion both male and female are
equal in companionship and intelligence. A dog is usually
considered to take a little longer to house train. Bitches do,
of course, come into season twice a year, immediately
becoming a great attraction to all males in the vicinity, which
can be difficult if you live in a built-up area. A bitch can of
course be spayed and if done early enough, ie after the first

season, will not have any effect on her character or temperament.

When buying a pet of any breed it is always better to buy from the actual breeder. Although many pet shops sell very good stock, if you buy from the breeder you will be able to judge the way the puppy has been raised and you will be allowed to see the puppy's mother which will give you some idea of how the puppy will look as an adult. Any breeder of repute will be only too pleased to answer any questions and will show you the litter with pride.

You will also be questioned on your suitability to own one of the puppies. Do not be upset by these questions, they nearly always prove the breeder cares about the puppy's future welfare as much as you care about buying a healthy happy puppy.

A well reared healthy puppy will always be friendly, with clear eyes, clean pink ears with no discharge from the ears and a clean white sparkling coat.

LOOKING AFTER YOUR PUPPY

When you have selected a puppy and before you leave ask the breeder for a diet sheet with the quantities, type of food and times of feeding the puppy has been used to. If you can keep to its diet for the first few days while it is settling in you will reduce the chance of an upset tummy due to a sudden change in diet. A few other details are also required. Ask for the puppy's Kennel Club registration, the pedigree with its date of birth and the date it was last wormed.

It is a wise precaution to take the puppy as soon after purchase as possible to your vet for a general health check and at the same time arrange for its first inoculations which must be done as soon as the vet recommends. Young puppies must not be allowed with other dogs or allowed on the streets or in parks until their full course of inoculations has been completed. Usually this course of injections will be completed by the time they are fourteen weeks.

Preparations

Before bringing the puppy home you will need to make a few preparations. It will need a bed, a feeding bowl, a water bowl, a comb and brush and a soft collar and lead. The bed can be a strong cardboard box with one side cut down—there is little use in buying a basket or bed at this stage as the puppy will undoubtedly chew it to pieces when teething. A cardboard box can be renewed when necessary, but make sure that the box is not held together with staples that would hurt the puppy. Line the box with a nice warm blanket or an old jumper, and put the box in a quiet draught-free corner out of the family's way. Both the water and feeding bowls require a good firm base; fresh water must be available at all times. Young puppies will not require much grooming but if they get used to a comb and brush from an early age they will always accept grooming without protest. The soft collar and lead will make it easier when training them in the garden. A strong collar and lead will be necessary once they can be taken walking in public places.

It is easy to understand how strange and frightened a puppy will feel on its first arrival in your home. Until now it has always been in close company with its litter mates and will be quite unused to being on its own. It must, however, very quickly learn to obey. Always use a very stern voice when it does wrong and a kind gentle voice when giving praise. A puppy will fall off if left on a chair or table because it is used to being on the ground, so always keep a firm hand on it. Young children should only be allowed to hold a very young puppy while sitting on the floor—puppies have a great habit of giving a sudden leap and a small child would be unable to hold on to the puppy. Puppies are very quick, so be careful when opening or shutting doors. All electric plugs and wires must be kept out of the puppy's way.

The first night

The problem of the puppy's first night is always quite difficult to solve. On its own for the first time it will feel not only frightened but rather cold and lonely and, unless you are very lucky, it will voice its misery by howling long and loud. You then have the choice of leaving it alone in the hope that it will tire itself out or else of taking it up to your bedroom which, unless you are prepared for it to sleep in your room for all time, is unsatisfactory. A fairly warm stone, *not* rubber, hot water bottle wrapped in a blanket and a well wrapped ticking clock put in its bed will compensate somewhat for its missing brothers and sisters. If it still complains do not go into the room, knock on the door and scold it. After a few nights it will accept its bed and bedtime quite happily.

If possible surround the puppy's bed with a pen similar to a child's play-pen which is big enough to enable one to leave plenty of newspaper outside the bed, so the puppy can relieve itself on waking, for puppies rarely soil their beds. The pen, which should have fine mesh sides high enough to prevent the puppy climbing out, is also very useful if the puppy has to be left on its own, for it will be safe and secure with its bed and toys. These pens can be bought at any good pet shop or made at home.

Diet

There are several things which are important and are worth remembering. Do keep all dog dishes absolutely clean. If the food is not eaten within ten minutes do not be tempted to leave it down for the puppy to eat later. There are two reasons for not leaving food down: first, a dog should be encouraged to eat its food quickly, which it will learn to do if, after a short time, it is removed and, second, any food left down will attract flies which will contaminate the food often causing gastro-enteritis at the worst or an upset stomach at the least, both of which are easily avoided with a little care.

Puppies up to the age of approximately six months require four meals a day. Always feed at the same time each day, so organise the meals to fit in with the family's timetable. It really doesn't matter what times you choose, providing they are the same each day.

Breakfast A little crushed plain cereal, such as Weetabix or cornflakes, moistened with warm milk. Twice a week a little scrambled egg with toast is appreciated.

Mid-day 3 to 4 oz cooked or raw meat, chicken, rabbit or fish, remove all bones.

Tea-time A drink of warm milk and a crushed digestive biscuit.

Dinner Similar to lunch.

A digestive biscuit at bedtime is appreciated.

Fresh water must always be available and never leave the bowl in the sun. Never ever give cooked bones because a cooked bone will splinter. A raw beef shin bone, however, is good for the puppy's teeth and will not splinter and can be safely given from eight weeks of age. Commercial dog foods, if fed according to instructions on the label, are usually satisfactory, although a vitamin supplement for growing puppies is to be recommended.

After a meal the puppy must always be allowed to rest for at least 15 minutes. Put the puppy outside as soon as it wakes as it will always relieve itself after sleeping. Stay with it until it does so and then praise it lavishly.

Daily care

GROOMING

Get your puppy used to daily grooming—it will always enjoy this routine if started from a very early age. Train it to lie on its side while you hold it down gently and always keep one hand on it. It will be easier for you both if you use a table that is an appropriate height for you.

Working from the shoulder towards the hindquarters, part and section the hair along the length of the puppy's body. Then brush and comb it, working from the tummy upwards. Make sure you rest your hand on the skin as you groom and part each section, otherwise the comb will pull the skin and cause discomfort. Pick any mats apart with your fingers. When you have finished one side, do the other. When grooming is complete praise the puppy. Do, however, keep these early sessions short, at this stage the important point is to get the puppy used to the grooming routine rather than the grooming itself.

BATHING

The puppy should be bathed once a fortnight. Always make sure the coat is free of mats and tangles. If you bath it when its coat is matted the mats will become quite impossible to remove without the aid of scissors. Take particular care with the coat under the ears and between the front legs, as these two areas seem to mat very quickly. After placing a small piece of cotton wool in each ear, stand the puppy on a rubber mat in a bath or basin, wet it completely using a mixer spray and warm water then shampoo well all over, taking great care not to get soap in its eyes. Rinse thoroughly and repeat. Make sure all soap is removed, for any left in the coat can cause irritation and will also leave the coat looking dead and lifeless. Towel dry then dry a small area at a time using a hair dryer set at medium heat and brushing each area with a soft pin or bristle brush. Once completely dry comb right through.

NAILS

Hold the foot firmly and using strong nail clippers cut each nail with care, stopping before you reach the quick which on white nails is pink. If you cut into the quick it will bleed. Black nails are a little harder to cut as the quick is hidden, just cut a little at a time until you see the quick. If you are worried about doing this, get your vet to do it. File the rough edges with an emery board or steel nail file.

If you intend to show your Bichon Frisé it will need to learn extra skills. It must walk well on your left side so that judges can see how it moves (*above*). And when set up for the judge (*below*), it must hold that position for as long as necessary.

Gertrude Fournier, doyenne of the Bichon Frisé world in the USA, judging at an English show, with the best dog and best bitch puppies to whom she has just presented awards.

Ch Sibon Fatal Attraction at Pamplona, Pengorse Poldark of Tresilva ex Ch Sibon Jasmyn (page 120), Best of Breed at Crufts 1990.

EARS

Gently remove any hair growing down into the ear with your fingers. Never probe into the inner ear, just remove the hairs you can see and dust sparingly with baby powder.

TRIMMING

Trim all hair that falls over the eyes. Scissor all wispy hair, making the coat an even length all over. This trimming will encourage the coat to grow and prevent any tendency for it to part down the back. Trim hair around the bottom of the feet. Do not scissor the tail, ears, moustache or beard, all of which must be treated with great care as the coat in these areas should be as long as possible. A puppy does not, of course, really need trimming but, again, let it become familiar with the scissors and the way it should stand so that later trimming sessions are easier.

TRAINING

The first essential in training a puppy is patience and understanding on your part. On its arrival at your home do remember that everything will be strange and rather frightening and the puppy will be overawed by all the new experiences, the strange noises and different surroundings. Nevertheless it is important for its welfare that it learns a few things quite quickly. Of these, its name and housetraining are probably the most essential.

Learning its name

The puppy must learn to recognise its name and to come when called. Call it by name and reward it with a tit-bit when it comes. Do this several times and it will soon know its name and you will have established the first step in training. *Never* call a puppy for unpleasant reasons. It is important that when it answers your call it is associated only with pleasant experiences, in this way it will always come when you call which can be important for its protection and your peace of mind.

Learning commands

As dogs understand and respond to tone of voice more than
the actual words, it is important, when they do wrong, that
the word 'No' is given in a firm and cross-sounding voice.
Equally, when they are obedient always use a kind and happy
voice. This applies especially to puppies.

House-training

All puppies have an instinct to be clean. If they have been
raised in a clean environment where they have been able to
leave their beds to relieve themselves on the paper provided
for that purpose they will rarely soil their beds, even from
the early age of three weeks. You must realise, however, that
a puppy has very little control, so it is up to you to make
sure it is taught the right spot from the beginning. The right
spot can be newspaper put down in the same place whenever
the puppy is running free in the house or a spot in the
garden. The first signs that a puppy wishes to relieve itself
are always the same: it will start to circle round sniffing the
floor. When you see it doing this, pick it up and, if the
weather permits, take it outside or place it on the newspaper.
In either case you must stay with the puppy until it does
what is required. If you leave it it will only follow you, so a
few minutes spent with it will be more successful. Remember
to praise the puppy when all is well.

Puppies should be taken to the right spot immediately after
waking and after meals. If, from the earliest moments, a
puppy has been taught to use newspaper this training can be
of great benefit to people living in flats when bad weather
makes it impossible to take the usual walk.

Please do not expect a puppy to be completely house-
trained straight away. You will undoubtedly get the
occasional mishap, after all, grass, carpet and paper probably
seem much the same to a puppy. Any stain can be removed
by swiftly applying soda water, leaving it for a few seconds
and then soaking it up with a tissue or paper towel.

Before leaving the matter of house-training, a puppy must also be trained to behave when in public places. So train it always to use the gutter. If an accident occurs this must be removed immediately, a plastic bag and rubber band will enable you to do this quickly and cleanly: put your hand in the bag, scoop up the excrement, turn the bag inside out and secure it with the elastic band.

Lead-training

Serious lead-training should not be attempted until your puppy is at least 12 weeks of age, but it is a good idea to get the puppy used to wearing a collar as soon as possible. A small cat collar can be useful but a soft leather collar is preferable. Once the puppy becomes used to its collar you can start lead training.

Start training in the garden, attach the lead and go where the puppy wants. Do not try to restrict it, just let it wander. Once it becomes aware that it is no longer free it will start to pull and strain, now drop the lead and let the puppy wander on its own with the lead trailing. After a few minutes pick up the lead and gently pull the lead towards you, calling the puppy's name as you do so. When it comes towards you reward it with a tit-bit. Do this several times. Once the puppy comes willingly, pull gently on the lead and encourage it to follow you. When it does, praise and reward it with a tit-bit. At first you will get the occasional objection, but if you are patient it will soon get the idea. One word of warning: do not let a puppy wander around with a loose lead unless you are watching, a lead can be quite dangerous if it gets caught and tangled in some object in the garden.

When the puppy is fully lead-trained in the garden and ready for its first outing do remember the noise of traffic and people will at first be quite frightening, so always make sure the collar and lead are strong and safe. The collar should be tight enough to stop the head slipping out if the puppy pulls backwards in fear, but not so tight it restricts the throat.

5 The Mature Bichon Frisé

The Bichon Frisé is considered to be fully mature at 12 months. By this time it will be fully grown and the second teeth will have erupted completely. The coat will have matured, although it is often thought that the adult coat is at its best later—it is often nearer to two years before it comes into full bloom.

Feeding

Once fully grown one meal a day is sufficient, but fed at the same time every day. The quantity of food will vary according to how much exercise and energy the dog expends. It is usually thought that 20 grams per 500 grams (¾ oz per 17½ oz) of body weight is about right and although protein is generally considered to be the main essential in the canine diet, the Bichon Frisé appears to fare better on a low protein diet.

Ch Kynismar Black Eyed Boogaloo, bred and owned by Mrs Atkins and an excellent example of a mature Bichon Frisé.

GENERAL COAT CARE

Because the Bichon Frisé does not shed its coat a daily grooming is far the most satisfactory way of preventing mats. Use a slicker brush to remove all dead hair, starting at the hair tip and working down to the roots. Remove any tangles with care. Take particular care to comb under the arms, down the legs and under the ears. This grooming is particularly essential in spring and autumn when the Bichon Frisé is changing its coat, otherwise in no time at all you will have a solid mat that can only be removed by stripping off the entire coat which will take a very long time to regrow. Grooming is dealt with in greater detail on page 71–77. To keep the Bichon Frisé looking its best don't let it get too dirty before you give it a bath (see page 72).

To prevent eye staining bathe under the eyes both in the morning and at night, using cotton wool squeezed out in warm water. Always remember to wipe its beard after it has eaten.

EXERCISE

Although the Bichon Frisé is a small dog it is remarkably sturdy and will enjoy as much exercise as many a bigger dog. Bichons Frisés that live in the country have been known to follow horses and even to catch the occasional rabbit. A quick walk is really quite inadequate—it needs room to run, jump and play, thereby exercising all its muscles. You have only to watch a Bichon Frisé rushing around the garden to know that this is the type of exercise it prefers. The amount of exercise can be safely left to it, because as soon as it is tired out it will rest.

TRAVEL

Unfortunately many dogs suffer from car sickness, which is distressing to both the dog and its owner. However, puppies introduced to car travel between seven and nine weeks of age rarely suffer from car sickness. It has been found that older Bichons Frisés prone to sickness are less likely to suffer if they travel in a well ventilated box or carrier with their vision restricted to forward only. The movement of the sky, bridges, pylons, lamp-posts or trees flashing by over their heads can upset them, causing both sickness and a fear of the car.

It is much safer for small dogs to travel in covered cages or travelling boxes. Many pet and novice owners consider it cruel to put dogs in these boxes, but they are mistaken. When provided with a box or cage made comfortable with a blanket in winter or a towel in the summer all dogs come to regard the box as their own special territory. At home leave the box around with the door open and you will find that your dog will probably retire voluntarily to the box when it needs a rest. On long car journeys in its familiar box the dog will feel safe and relaxed and the driver can be secure in the knowledge that the dog is well protected in the case of a sudden stop, or any other eventuality.

The travelling cage, with a cover, or the travelling box will prove invaluable for transporting your beautifully groomed Bichon Frisé from the car to the show bench. If it is cold or raining the dog will keep warm, dry and clean.

The size of the box or cage is important: it must be large enough for a Bichon Frisé to stand up and turn around.

The Parked Car

Many owners do not realise how dangerous it is to leave their dogs in parked cars. With quickly changing weather which can alter from cloud and rain to bright sunshine in a very short time, and the sun's movement changing a cool shady spot into a sun-drenched one, the heat in a car's interior can increase drastically in a very short time. A slightly open window is of little use once the sun shines on to the car. On a really sunny day even with the car windows wide open it can still become far too hot. The car's interior can heat to a temperature of 50°C/120°F or more. At these temperatures a dog cannot breathe and will sink into a coma.

Death can then occur very quickly. Each year many dogs die in this way.

GROOMING

The coat of the Bichon Frisé is quite different from that of any other breed of dog. It is a dense soft coat and becomes very curly if left to dry naturally. However, for the showring, the dog is bathed and the coat blow-dried, brushed and scissored to give the 'powder-puff' effect. This effect was perfected by the first Bichon Frisé exhibitors in the USA, and has been responsible for the breed's success in both the showring and as a pet.

Preparation should begin at a very early age, particularly if you intend to show your dog, for this will ensure that the coat is in first-class condition by the time you are ready to trim it for exhibition. First study your dog's outline: does it look too short on leg? too long in back? has it a good reach of neck? It is obviously silly to make the dog look even longer in back by leaving too much hair on the chest and rump, scissoring under the body if rather leggy or not scissoring when short on leg. Scissoring can improve and enhance the Bichon Frisé's outline, so study your dog well before trimming. A good photograph of a well-presented Bichon is a great help, and so is a mirror placed in such a way that you can see the outline of the dog.

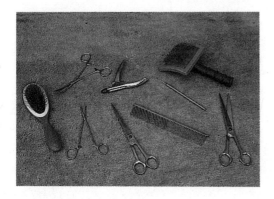

1 Equipment. Curved scissors, nail clippers, slicker brush, tooth scaler, pair of scissors with long blades, pair of scissors with short blades, comb, bristle brush.

2 Comb through coat thoroughly, removing all mats. Stand dog on mat in bath, using spray wet coat all over.

3 Protect eyes, put a small piece of cotton wool in each ear. Shampoo the coat thoroughly.

4 Wash legs and feet and under the body.

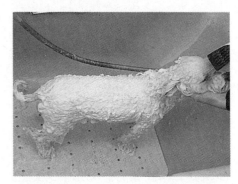

5 Rinse coat at least twice, apply conditioner and rinse again.

6 With a warm towel dry off all surplus water.

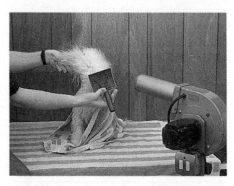

7 Blow dry a small section at a time brushing the coat upwards and outwards as it dries.

8 When completely dry comb the coat out and up away from the skin.

9 Always hold scissors flat on the coat to scissor.
10 Comb coat up and scissor straight along the back from tail to withers.

11 Lift dog up while scissoring underneath.

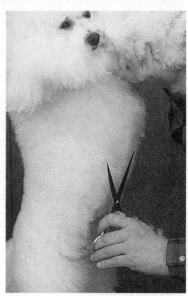

12 Hold ears and moustache while scissoring the chest. When scissoring the front legs keep them cylindrical, removing excess hair between legs.

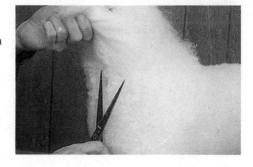

13 Work around under ears and over the shoulder curving towards the withers.
14 Use curved scissors under brisket and create a gradual curve from the elbow up to the flank.

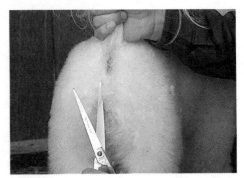

15 Scissor a straight line down the outside of each leg so when viewed from the rear each outer leg is vertical.

16 Remove excess hair between rear legs, shape leg to show angulation.
17 Cut front of rear leg straight.

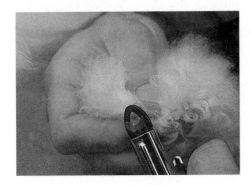

18 To cut hold nail firmly between thumb and finger.

19 Comb the hair down over the feet. Cut all hair falling below the level of the pad and excess hair between pads.

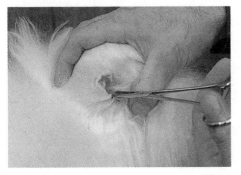

20 Remove excess hair in the ear gently, but do not probe into the ear.

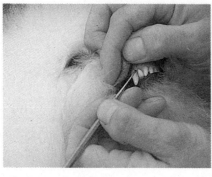

21 Use scaler to remove tartar and to clean teeth, be careful not to cut the gums.
22 Comb hair up on top-knot.
23 Comb hair down over ears.

24 With dog facing you scissor the top-knot into a semi-circle including the hair on the ears. From the side scissor in a gradual curve from top of head down to withers.

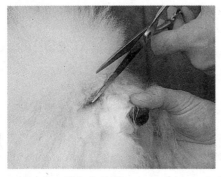

25 Scissor all hair falling over the eyes, hold scissors parallel, keep points well away from the eyes.
26 Using curved scissors and the centre of the blades, clear the hair at the corner of the eyes.

27 To protect the moustache of a show Bichon Frisé wrap it in a small square of tissue paper and secure with a small rubber band.

28 The finished head.

29 Ready for the show.

THE OLD DOG

Bichons Frisés will, of course, vary, but in good health and well cared for they often live to quite a good age—between 11 and 13 years is the average. But there will come a time when it is obvious that life has lost its meaning. The Bichon Frisé with its white coat does not show its age as quickly as dogs with black or dark coats whose muzzles often turn grey as they get older. Probably the first sign of age in the Bichon Frisé is a slowing of movement. But there are other clues: it may not see too well, or it suffers from a loss of hearing, and the coat often becomes thin and sparse. None of these things may bother it, especially when kept warm and out of draughts with good food given regularly. It is only when the dog is in constant pain that a loving owner must consult the vet and make the decision to give his/her faithful pet and companion of many years a quick and painless relief from suffering and a life without meaning. It is the final act of kindness you owe your pet.

6 Exhibiting the Bichon Frisé

CHOOSING

When you consider the attractiveness of all puppies at eight weeks of age, and especially the Bichon Frisé, it is easy to understand how difficult it is for even the most experienced breeder to guarantee a particular puppy as 'show' quality until it reaches the age of six months. After all from eight weeks of age so many things can alter: the muzzle can grow longer, the eyes can lighten, it can grow too long in back or become too leggy, the coat can become coarse, sparse or too straight and the second teeth can change the bite which may then become undershot or overshot, or it might grow too big or for that matter remain too small. Any of these points could be a drawback in the showring for the mature Bichon Frisé, although an undershot or overshot jaw is quite unacceptable.

It is possible to buy from an experienced breeder a promising puppy—a puppy that looks a potential show specimen. However, it really is, at this age, a matter of luck. Many a promising puppy has become just a pet and many a pet puppy has turned out to be of show quality. If you wish to buy a top quality Bichon Frisé wait until you can buy one at least six months old, for only at that age can you and the breeder be sure that it is of show quality. Here are a few hints which could be a help if you are looking for a promising show puppy.

• Do ask the breeder to let you see the mother of the litter from which you are making your selection, any obvious faults in her may very easily come out in one or two of her puppies.

A puppy with show potential—it is standing well and holding its tail correctly. But it is extremely difficult, even for experienced breeders, to know if a puppy will maintain its promise.

- Make sure that all the litter are of a friendly and outgoing nature.
- Ask the breeder to divide the sexes and for a short while just study the puppies of the sex you require, taking note of their general behaviour and movement.
- For a closer examination stand the puppy on a firm table, always keeping a hand on it as puppies have a habit of jumping very quickly and have no idea of height or distance. The muzzle should be short at this age and the skull behind the eyes should be broad. The ears should be set just above eye level, with the leathers, which are thin, reaching half way down the muzzle, the inner ear pink and clean smelling. Look for dark, round, fairly large eyes, forward looking and

Ch Leijazulip Kipling of Sha-maney has the dark nose, lips, eye-rims and haloes so essential in any good Bichon Frisé.

well spaced with a keen and intelligent expression. A scissor bite is essential and the teeth should be white and even with tight black lips.

• The body should feel firm. The puppy should have a nice reach of neck, the back should be level with a high set tail which is carried curved but not touching the back, make sure the tail is quite straight without any kink or bend. The front legs should be quite straight when viewed from the front. The back legs should have a good bend of stifle. Feet should be tight and round with well cushioned pads.

• The pigment on the nose, lips, eye-rims and pads must be black. The skin over the inner corner of the eyes should also be well pigmented. This area of dark skin is referred to as the 'halo' and without these haloes the true Bichon Frisé expression is quite lost.

• The puppy coat is rather difficult to judge but a thin sparse coat or a coat of a coarse texture should be avoided. Look for a thick dense fairly long curly coat.

• Puppies are quite often born with apricot or beige mark-ings on the ears and parts of the body, but providing these are fairly pale they will usually fade as the puppy matures.

• Temperament must be outgoing and friendly.

• If selecting a male make certain that it is entire with two testicles descended into the scrotum.

TRAINING FOR THE SHOWRING

The Bichon Frisé is very intelligent and has a strong desire to please, so is very quick to learn. The first essential is to get the puppy used to noise and crowds. You can start this part of the training as soon as it has been inoculated. One of the best ways is to take it shopping with you. If you travel by car all the better as this will enable it to get used to car travel at the same time. After each journey give it a run or a walk so that it will come to associate the car with pleasant outings. From experience I have found that if puppies get used to the car from the very first, ie eight weeks, they rarely suffer from car sickness.

Once it is used to meeting people, every time someone comes to the house ask them to go over the puppy. Place it on a table and get each visitor to run their hands over its body and gently open the mouth to look at the teeth.

Next teach the puppy to stand without moving. Give the command 'Stay' and leave it for a brief moment, then reward it with a tit-bit. Carry out this routine each day, gradually extending the 'stay' period, but each time remembering to give a reward.

All show dogs have to walk in a triangle for the judge to assess their movement, so it is wise to teach the puppy this procedure in the garden. Set up a square ring and, with the puppy on your left side, walk it up and down and around in a triangle and in a circle. Don't let it pull or jump up, but encourage it to move steadily at your side, always praising and rewarding it when it moves correctly.

Finally you must learn how to set your dog in its best position for the judge's approval. To place the front legs in their correct position lift the dog's head so its feet are just off the ground. When you release the head the legs will come down quite parallel, with the feet turning neither in nor out. Then place the rear legs so they are also parallel and not too close together. Now, with the collar up just under the ears, hold the lead taut with one hand and with the other make sure the tail is kept over the back. Give the command 'Stay'.

The above training is really all you can achieve at home, so it would be to your advantage to take the puppy to a training class. These classes are held in most areas and your vet will know of those held locally. At training classes you will be able to accustom your puppy to the presence of other dogs both large and small. To a Bichon Frisé puppy a Great Dane or German Shepherd dog must be an awesome and rather frightening sight when first encountered, but after a short while the puppy will become quite used to all the various breeds which it will undoubtedly meet once it starts its show career.

DOG SHOWS
All dog shows in the United Kingdom come under the jurisdiction of the Kennel Club. The Kennel Club registration of your puppy will have been taken care of by the breeder, as mentioned in Chapter 4, and it should now be transferred into your name. No dog can be entered in any show unless it is registered at the KC. Every week practically without exception many shows licensed by the KC are held up and down the country. The two weekly dog papers *Dog World* and *Our Dogs* both advertise these events. Before deciding which show to enter here is a brief description of the different types of show.

Championship Shows

First and foremost are the great Championship Shows, of which Crufts is the best known. Each year there are 27 Championship Shows which cater for all the breeds registered at the Kennel Club. It is at these shows that the KC Challenge Certificates are awarded by the judge to the best dog and best bitch in each breed. To obtain the title of Champion a dog/bitch must win three of these Challenge Certificates under three different judges—not an easy task because in most breeds the number of top winning dogs in the country can vary between 100 and 250 dogs. Champion-

Eng and Ir Ch Tiopepi Mad Louie at Pamplona posing for photographs with Geoff Cornish (left), his handler, and Andrew Brace, the judge, after winning at the Southern Counties Canine Championship show. Owner: Michael Coad.

ship shows, often held over four days, are the only events where these certificates are on offer, which makes them the most important occasions in the dog calendar.

Open Shows

These are more relaxed affairs and as the name suggests are open to all. They vary very much in size from 150 classes upwards and are usually limited to breeds which the society running the show considers will draw a good entry in their area. Open Shows held outdoors on a pleasant day in the summer are always good places to introduce a young puppy to the exciting world of the show dog.

Limited Shows

All exhibitors must be members of the club holding this type of show, which is often held in the afternoon or evening.

They are pleasant occasions without any very serious competition, so are also good places for a puppy's first outing.

Exemption Shows

These are the only shows which provide classes for unregistered or cross-bred dogs. Often held in aid of a charity they are 'fun' events and are used by many an experienced exhibitor to accustom their young puppies to walking around a ring, standing on a table and meeting other breeds. In addition to the 'fun' classes these shows always provide four classes for pedigree dogs.

The first outing to a dog show is always an ordeal for a puppy, so it is wise to select a show fairly close to the puppy's home. A long journey plus the excitement of its first show can prove too much for some puppies. One of the smaller shows listed above, not too far away, is an excellent place to begin.

NOTES FOR THE NOVICE

When your puppy is six months of age and if it is happy and outgoing, looking in first-class condition with a fairly good coat, is used to the lead and has learnt the rudiments of show training, you can start thinking about entering it for a few shows.

By studying the list of shows published in the dog press every week you will be able to choose a show fairly close to where you live. These shows are advertised well in advance so you will have plenty of time to phone or write to the secretary for a schedule. The schedule contains a definition of classes, an entry form and the names of all the breeds and the classes allocated to them. On receipt of the schedule choose which class or classes you wish to enter. It is best not to tire a puppy too much, so one or two classes are usually enough.

Fill in the entry form with care, enclose the right entrance fee and send it back to the secretary before the closing date which is always printed in the schedule.

On the front of the schedule, which you should take with you to the show, make a note of the classes you have entered. This may seem unnecessary, but it is very easy to forget, especially when you start to show regularly and, at the busiest time of the year, shows come in rapid succession. Make a special note if you enter more than one dog.

Most exhibitors keep a special bag for all the necessary items needed at the show. You will need a benching blanket, a small water bowl, a show lead (a nylon show lead is best for the Bichon Frisé, but if your puppy has been used to a leather collar and lead use it for the first few shows, then gradually get it used to a nylon lead), comb, brush, scissors and grooming powder, tit-bits, kitchen towel, plastic bags to remove any excreta, rubber bands to secure same, a flask of coffee and a box of sandwiches complete the list. Keep the schedule, which often includes the route to the show, your passes and ring numbers if sent, in your handbag.

Be prepared for all types of weather. Most seasoned exhibitors keep in their cars everything they need for fine or wet, hot or cold weather, especially for the outdoor shows.

You also need to think about what you will wear. The Bichon Frisé always shows up better against dark-coloured clothing. Full flowing skirts detract from the dog, close fitting slacks or skirts are better. High-heeled shoes are a menace, indoors they make a loud noise and can frighten other dogs, out of doors they sink in the ground. Flat shoes are far more suitable both indoors and out.

Your Bichon Frisé, being very intelligent, will know as soon as the day arrives that there is excitement in the air, so do try not to rush. Get up early, giving yourself plenty of time to have a cup of tea or coffee and load the car, thereby giving the puppy ample time to relieve itself before setting off on the journey.

On arrival at the show ground buy a catalogue and then find your bench. Although toy breeds are supplied with cages at the Championship Shows, at other shows you may find either a bench or cage with your number on. Make the bench or cage comfortable with the blanket and secure the puppy either by its lead, which must not be too long, or by closing the cage securely. An added protection is to tie the lead around the door. Once you have unpacked and set up your grooming table in the area provided, take the puppy for a slow walk around the show ground giving it time to become acclimatised to the general noise and atmosphere. At the same time you can ascertain which ring has been allocated for your breed.

When your class is called go into the ring slowly, set your puppy up in the correct position as practised at home, listen to the judge, move as the judge requests and stay in the position he/she puts you. Once the judge has selected the winners, and if you are not amongst them, congratulate the winner and leave the ring quietly.

One's first show is always somewhat overwhelming to both puppy and owner, but at these shows you will be able to learn more about the Bichon Frisé from other exhibitors. In addition you will enjoy a day among people who are all dedicated to our friend the dog.

7 Breeding

DOMINANT AND RECESSIVE GENES

All puppies receive 50% of their genetic material from each parent, so by delving into the ancestry of a Bichon Frisé it is possible to evaluate the dog's genetic pattern as a whole.

Characteristics controlled by dominant genes always appear if the genes are present in the dog's genetic make-up. On the other hand, a characteristic controlled by a recessive gene will be masked by a characteristic controlled by a dominant gene. Therefore it is easy to understand that the breeding value of a Bichon Frisé, or indeed any animal, cannot be assessed on appearance alone.

The following is a list of dominant and recessive traits which, according to research, seem to apply to the Bichon Frisé. This list shows that desirable features come from both dominant and recessive genes, which makes breeding top quality dogs that much more difficult!

Dominant	Recessive
Thick coat	Sparse coat
Large ears	Short ears
Low-set ears	High-set ears
Heavy bone	Light bone
Large round eyes	Small eyes
Dark eyes	Light eyes
Deep chest	Lack of rib cage
Short muzzle	Long muzzle
Short neck	Long neck
Upright shoulder	Well laid shoulder
Black pigment	Pure white coat
Scissor bite	Undershot jaw
Good movement	Overshot jaw

Any dog carrying a dominant trait will show it. A recessive trait can be carried unseen but when a dog with a recessive trait is mated to another with the same recessive trait, that trait will appear in about 25% of the puppies. Thus in a litter of four puppies one may be clear, two may be carriers and one may show the recessive trait.

In an effort to make this difficult subject more simple let us suppose that we have a Bichon Frisé with a short muzzle (a dominant trait) mated to a Bichon Frisé with an equally short muzzle. If neither carry the recessive gene for a long muzzle all their puppies will have short muzzles. If only one of this pair is a carrier of the recessive gene, the puppies will still all have short muzzles. However, if both the pair carry the unseen recessive gene for long muzzles their puppies will have long muzzles in a ratio of 1 in 4. If both sire and dam have long muzzles, all the puppies will have long muzzles.

A dominant gene can be lost, but a recessive one never is. This principle goes for all dominant and recessive genes.

DOMINANT TRAITS
- affect a large number of a dog's progeny
- are always visible in an animal
- will reduce any danger of continuing unwanted traits
- never skip a generation
- will guarantee the breeding pattern

RECESSIVE TRAITS
- can skip a generation
- must be carried by both sire and dam to be apparent
- a dog carrying a pair will exhibit the trait
- a dog carrying only one will not exhibit the trait.

To sum up, if a dog carries a dominant trait, then that trait, good or bad, is always visible. If a dog carries a recessive trait then, whether the trait is good or bad, it is not always visible.

INBREEDING

This is the mating of closely related animals: son to mother, father to daughter, half-brother to half-sister and, closest of all, brother to sister.

Inbreeding creates neither faults nor virtues, it simply fixes them in the progeny. Inbreeding concentrates both good features *and* bad faults. It can strengthen dominant traits and will always reveal recessive ones, thereby giving the breeder control in combining and balancing similar genetic factors. Inbreeding is not considered to produce any degeneration, it simply concentrates faults and weaknesses already present, thus enabling the breeder to recognise and eradicate them in future breeding plans. From this it follows that it is of the greatest importance that any breeder adopting this method uses animals which are as perfect as possible.

LINE-BREEDING

Line-breeding has proved highly successful in breeding pro-grammes. Line-breeding entails the selection of breeding stock who have one or more common ancestors of outstanding worth. Line-breeding to an outstanding individual in the pedigree will help to improve the strain and is not as 'intensive' as inbreeding.

OUTCROSSING

The mating of two unrelated animals (outcrossing) is always a bit of a gamble. Breeding like to like should, and often does, produce puppies similar to their parents but outcrossing for one virtue will often bring unwanted faults as well.

MATING YOUR BICHON FRISÉ

Generally speaking the mating of dogs and bitches should be left in the hands of experienced breeders. It can be very difficult for the pet owner to be sure, when mating their bitch, that the stud dog is the right sire, and that sound and healthy puppies will result from the mating. It is only with a good knowledge of the genetic background of both dog and bitch that a breeder can be pretty sure that the result of such a mating will produce good stock. If the owner of a pet bitch really wants to let it have a litter, the best thing to do is to go back to the breeder who will be able to assist in the right choice of a sire and will often be willing to help when the puppies are born.

Bichon Frisé bitches usually come into season when fairly young, often at six months. At this time the bitch is still only a puppy, but by the second season she is much more mature. As a general rule the earliest a bitch should be allowed to produce a litter is when she is over 12 months of age. Any breeder whose bitch produces a litter before she has reached full maturity is more likely to be interested in the commercial outcome of a litter than the welfare of the bitch.

When considering all the implications of allowing your bitch to be mated do not overlook how much time you will have to allocate to the litter once weaning commences and the puppies are running free, which will start at about three weeks of age and continue until you have found safe and happy homes for them at eight weeks. Many owners will find this period in the puppies' lives very time-consuming and if they themselves lead a very busy life they must be sure someone will always be there at that time. Always think carefully before allowing any bitch to be mated.

Once the bitch comes in season, which will last about three weeks, you must inform the owner of the selected stud dog. The time of mating depends entirely on the bitch. It is often considered that bitches are ready for mating between the 10th and 15th day or when the colour of the discharge fades. This, however, is not always a good guide because some bitches show a red discharge throughout their season. The best way to ensure a fertile mating is to watch the actions of the bitch. The only sure time is when the bitch indicates that she is ready, which she will do by standing rigid with tail to one side when in the company of other bitches. Another good sign is a softening of the vulva. If, at this time, the bitch is scratched on her back just above her

MATING & WHELPING CHART

based on the bitch carrying her litter for 62 days

Mated January	To whelp March	Mated February	To whelp April	Mated March	To whelp May	Mated April	To whelp June	Mated May	To whelp July	Mated June	To whelp Aug.	Mated July	To whelp Sept.	Mated August	To whelp Oct.	Mated Sept.	To whelp Nov.	Mated October	To whelp Dec.	Mated Nov.	To whelp Jan.	Mated Dec.	To whelp Feb.
1	5	1	5	1	3	1	3	1	3	1	3	1	2	1	3	1	3	1	3	1	3	1	2
2	6	2	6	2	4	2	4	2	4	2	4	2	3	2	4	2	4	2	4	2	4	2	3
3	7	3	7	3	5	3	5	3	5	3	5	3	4	3	5	3	5	3	5	3	5	3	4
4	8	4	8	4	6	4	6	4	6	4	6	4	5	4	6	4	6	4	6	4	6	4	5
5	9	5	9	5	7	5	7	5	7	5	7	5	6	5	7	5	7	5	7	5	7	5	6
6	10	6	10	6	8	6	8	6	8	6	8	6	7	6	8	6	8	6	8	6	8	6	7
7	11	7	11	7	9	7	9	7	9	7	9	7	8	7	9	7	9	7	9	7	9	7	8
8	12	8	12	8	10	8	10	8	10	8	10	8	9	8	10	8	10	8	10	8	10	8	9
9	13	9	13	9	11	9	11	9	11	9	11	9	10	9	11	9	11	9	11	9	11	9	10
10	14	10	14	10	12	10	12	10	12	10	12	10	11	10	12	10	12	10	12	10	12	10	11
11	15	11	15	11	13	11	13	11	13	11	13	11	12	11	13	11	13	11	13	11	13	11	12
12	16	12	16	12	14	12	14	12	14	12	14	12	13	12	14	12	14	12	14	12	14	12	13
13	17	13	17	13	15	13	15	13	15	13	15	13	14	13	15	13	15	13	15	13	15	13	14
14	18	14	18	14	16	14	16	14	16	14	16	14	15	14	16	14	16	14	16	14	16	14	15
15	19	15	19	15	17	15	17	15	17	15	17	15	16	15	17	15	17	15	17	15	17	15	16
16	20	16	20	16	18	16	18	16	18	16	18	16	17	16	18	16	18	16	18	16	18	16	17
17	21	17	21	17	19	17	19	17	19	17	19	17	18	17	19	17	19	17	19	17	19	17	18
18	22	18	22	18	20	18	20	18	20	18	20	18	19	18	20	18	20	18	20	18	20	18	19
19	23	19	23	19	21	19	21	19	21	19	21	19	20	19	21	19	21	19	21	19	21	19	20
20	24	20	24	20	22	20	22	20	22	20	22	20	21	20	22	20	22	20	22	20	22	20	21
21	25	21	25	21	23	21	23	21	23	21	23	21	22	21	23	21	23	21	23	21	23	21	22
22	26	22	26	22	24	22	24	22	24	22	24	22	23	22	24	22	24	22	24	22	24	22	23
23	27	23	27	23	25	23	25	23	25	23	25	23	24	23	25	23	25	23	25	23	25	23	24
24	28	24	28	24	26	24	26	24	26	24	26	24	25	24	26	24	26	24	26	24	26	24	25
25	29	25	29	25	27	25	27	25	27	25	27	25	26	25	27	25	27	25	27	25	27	25	26
26	30	26	30	26	28	26	28	26	28	26	28	26	27	26	28	26	28	26	28	26	28	26	27
27	31			27	29	27	29	27	29	27	29	27	28	27	29	27	29	27	29	27	29	27	28
				28	30	28	30	28	30	28	30	28	29	28	30	28	30	28	30	28	30		
				29	31			29	31	29	31	29	30	29	31			29	31	29	31		

Mated January	To whelp April	Mated February	To whelp May	Mated March	To whelp June	Mated April	To whelp July	Mated May	To whelp Aug.	Mated June	To whelp Sept.	Mated July	To whelp Oct.	Mated August	To whelp Nov.	Mated Sept.	To whelp Dec.	Mated October	To whelp Jan.	Mated Nov.	To whelp Feb.	Mated Dec.	To whelp March
28	1	27	1	30	1	29	1	30	1	30	1	30	1	30	1	29	1	30	1	30	1	28	1
29	2	28	2	31	2	30	2	31	2			31	2	31	2	30	2	31	2			29	2
30	3	29	3																			30	3
31	4																					31	4

tail, and she is ready for mating, she will flag her tail to one side.

It is a wise precaution to give the bitch a worm tablet either just before or just after mating, as this will reduce the risk of high infestation in the puppies.

Although it is the usual practice for the bitch to visit the dog, it is often preferable if the dog can visit the bitch, especially if she is a maiden who will be more relaxed in her own surroundings. In any case it is important to allow both dog and bitch to play together before the mating takes place. They should be introduced to one another while they are on leads in case the bitch is unfriendly. Once you are sure there is no sign of aggression they can be released. In this way the mating will be more acceptable to the bitch. Many a mating is made difficult by too much interference by the owners, a natural mating is far better than a forced mating. When the dog mounts the bitch she should be held gently by the collar. Once the tie is established the dog will turn around and they will stand back to back. It is wise to steady them both until the dog withdraws.

Both dog and bitch should then be allowed to rest.

After the bitch's season is finished she should be treated quite normally. She will not require extra food until the fourth to fifth week, but all food must be of the highest quality with plenty of protein, and a mineral and vitamin supplement should be given daily. After the fifth week her appetite will increase. At this time it is advisable to feed twice a day. Foods rich in calcium, that is eggs, milk and cheese, should supplement the normal protein food in the last weeks before parturition.

EQUIPMENT
Once you are sure your bitch is in whelp you will need several items in preparation for the puppies' arrival.

The whelping box

First is the whelping box. This should be big enough for the bitch to lie in comfortably with enough space for the puppies. The box should have a front opening and a hinged lid. It should be placed in a warm, dry draught-free corner away from the family where it will be quiet and free from disturbance. It is wise to surround this box with some sort of enclosure to prevent the bitch carrying her puppies around the room—not a usual habit but it has been known. The bitch should become accustomed to this box well before her time. When heavy in whelp she will appreciate a soft bed in it, but when labour commences all bedding must be removed and the box lined with plenty of newspaper. Once the puppies are born you will need to put a low barrier across the box's opening, to prevent the puppies leaving the box, for while they are tiny they are unlikely to be able to find their way back.

Other items
- disinfectant in which to wash your hands before touching bitch or puppies
- clean rough towelling to stimulate and dry the puppies
- a puppy feeder in case the bitch is unable to feed her puppies. If this happens you will have to hand rear them using a feeder, which can be a premature baby bottle and teat or a special feeder used for kittens. Lactol and Whelpie are two foods manufactured especially for the needs of premature puppies and when fed strictly according to the directions are invaluable in such an emergency
- glucose to give to the bitch in milk both during and after labour
- an infra-red lamp or heating pad. Puppies require a high temperature at birth—between 75°–80°F (23°–26°C)

LABOUR
The first signs that your bitch is commencing labour is a restlessness and panting which will go on for roughly 24 hours. During this time she will scratch and tear up the paper in the whelping box. If you take her temperature, you will

see that it will have dropped below the normal body temperature of 101.5°F (54.7°C). All this activity is followed by a rather quiet period when the bitch will lie still or even go to sleep.

Labour pains will soon commence. At first they are quite far apart, but gradually get closer and closer until the water bag, which looks rather like a small brown balloon, appears. Within the hour this will burst and very shortly after the first puppy will appear. If the puppy does not appear within an hour of the water bag bursting or if the labour pains continue for longer than two hours or if they get weaker the vet should be called.

WHELPING
Once the first puppy is born the interval between the arrival of each one can vary. Quite often they arrive quickly one after the other, but any interval up to several hours is not unusual. If the bitch is quiet and resting there is no cause for concern, but if she is restless and appears to be straining for some time without a puppy appearing you should call your vet.

Puppies are often born feet first, referred to as a 'breech birth'. In the Bichon Frisé this is no cause for concern, it is only in breeds with large heads that a breech birth may cause difficulties.

After the whelping is over gently remove all soiled paper from the whelping box and replace with clean paper or, preferably, a Vetbed. It is always wise to get your vet to come and check that all is well with both the bitch and her puppies and any abnormalities in the puppies can be diagnosed immediately.

Whelping is a perfectly natural process and from experience I have found the Bichon Frisé to be a fairly easy whelper, so I strongly advise that she be allowed to produce her litter without interference. It is only when things appear to be abnormal that assistance should be given. Even maiden bitches know by instinct exactly the right way to open the sac, break the cord and wash the new-born puppy, the bitch will then expel the afterbirth which she will, if allowed, eat.

However, it is not unknown for a maiden bitch to be a little confused at the birth of the first whelp, so you need to keep a quiet, discreet eye on her. If she doesn't bite open the bag as soon as the puppy is born, you must release it at once. Open the bag with your fingers, so the puppy can take its first breath. As soon as the puppy is released instinct will prompt the bitch and she will take care of the rest. Any agitation or worry on your part will only disturb the bitch, so do stay cool and calm.

CARE OF NEW-BORN PUPPIES
After food warmth is the most important necessity for new-born puppies. It is vital that a temperature between 75°F and 80°F (23.9°C and 26.6°C) is maintained for at least the first few days. At birth puppies have a temperature between 94°F and 99°F (34.4°C and 37.2°C) which is much lower than the adult Bichon Frisé, and as the shivering reflex does not develop until the puppy is eight days old, it is essential to keep the puppies warm. The sucking reflex in healthy puppies is strong at birth, but if a puppy is weak or cold this reflex becomes weaker. Contented puppies are always quiet, any crying is usually a sign that all is not well, they are either cold or hungry, or both.

All puppies should double their birth weight in one week. The best way of ensuring puppies are gaining weight is to weigh them 24 hours after birth and once a day for the first two weeks. This will also help you check that even the smallest in the litter is progressing.

Carry out a daily check to make certain the bitch is keeping the puppies clean and that the whelping box is spotless. Renew the paper or put in a clean Vetbed whenever necessary.

If all goes well and the puppies are all thriving, on the fourth day but certainly before they are a week old, all dew claws should be removed. This can be done either by your vet or an experienced breeder. The bitch should be taken away from the puppies while this small operation is carried out. After seven days the puppies' nails will become very sharp and if not cut will cause the bitch quite a bit of discomfort, so do keep them well trimmed (see page 75).

The above is only a brief description of breeding and whelping. More detailed information will be found in the many books specialising in these subjects, some of which are listed in the Bibliography.

CARE OF PUPPIES FROM 3–8 weeks

Puppies are born with their eyes and ears closed. Some time between 12 and 16 days their eyes will open, and they must be protected from any bright light. Ears open at about the same time although their hearing will not become acute until the puppies are four weeks old.

Once their eyes are completely open the puppies will start to explore their surroundings. If they fall out of the whelping box and find it impossible to get back the bitch will become distressed, so the low slat used to keep them from falling out when tiny must now be removed, or a small step provided which the puppies will soon learn to climb over to return to their bed.

Weaning

When weaning should begin will very much depend on the size of the litter. If it is a big litter weaning should start at three weeks, otherwise four weeks is usually considered early enough, the puppies will still be getting an ample supply of milk from the bitch so this is the time to start. As this is one of the important phases in a puppy's life it is essential it is carried out without haste and equally essential that the right food in the right amount is given. If any diarrhoea occurs it is usually a case of too much too quickly.

Ideally, the puppies' introduction to solid food should be when they have just woken up and before they have had time

How Bichon Frisé puppies develop: at one day (*top left*), five days (*left*) and four weeks (*below*). Eyes start to open between 10 and 14 days, and the pale markings will fade as the puppies grow.

Overleaf Eng and Ir Ch Sulyka Snoopy, champion in 1984, Ch Leijazulip Jazz of Zudiki (page 116), ex Shamaney My Choice of Sulyka.

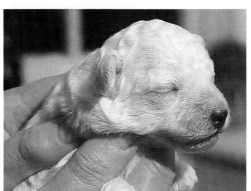

to feed from the bitch.

I have found the quickest way to introduce puppies to solid food is to start by giving them a tiny piece of butcher's raw scraped beef in your fingers. They will suck the meat at first but once tasted they will eat the rest with relish. Give one meat meal a day for three days, and then two a day.

As soon as they are used to the scraped beef they will quickly learn to lap up a warm milk meal. This may be cow's or goat's milk or one of the commercial brands prepared especially for weaning puppies. By the tenth day of this new regime they should be having two meat meals (about ½ oz (14g) each meal) and three milk meals (freshly prepared for each meal) a day.

Once the puppies are eating and drinking with ease a little scrambled egg or cereal can be mixed with the milk. As the puppies mature crushed up toasted wholemeal bread or a puppy meal can be added to both meat and milk meals.

The quantities given should be increased gradually. Once they are completely weaned all the puppies should be fed in separate dishes which will enable you to check that they are all eating well. Quantities will vary according to the size of the puppy. Meals should be provided four times a day and always at the same time.

During weaning the mother should be kept away from the puppies for longer and longer periods. Another of the bitch's natural instincts is often a surprise to owners: as the bitch's milk recedes she will, if near her puppies after she has eaten, regurgitate her food for her puppies. This will do no harm, providing she has not eaten any large lumps which may choke a puppy, but it will mean that she requires another meal. This regurgitation is best avoided by keeping the bitch away from her puppies for at least an hour after every meal.

Once weaning has commenced the mother will often be reluctant to keep the puppies or the bedding clean, so you must examine all the puppies to make sure they are quite clean on their faces and under their tails because both can become very dirty unless cleaned fairly frequently. Use cotton wool moistened in warm water for any cleaning. Puppies never soil their sleeping quarters so make sure there is plenty of paper just outside their sleeping area.

Worming

Puppies must be treated against roundworms at four weeks and thereafter at two week intervals until the age of three months. The medication should always be obtained from your vet.

Socialisation

From three to four weeks of age all puppies should be allowed to become accustomed to the daily household noises. It is also wise to get them used to being handled and talked to by all the family. Puppies reared in this way will never suffer from nerves—it is the isolated puppy who will find it difficult when later confronted with crowds and noise. As the puppies mature they will require more and more exercise which they will provide for themselves by wrestling and sparring with each other. Whenever the weather permits, fresh air and a free run in the garden are essential for their well-being.

Even at this very young age a light brushing and combing can be used with advantage (see page 69) because it will accustom them to grooming in the future.

8 Veterinary Care

Trevor Turner B. Vet Med. MR.CVS

The decision to share your home with a Bichon Frisé is in many ways wise, not least because, as a comparatively recently recognised breed, breeding is confined to quite small numbers of people who are intent on producing good puppies. Breeders are fully aware of the problems indiscriminate breeding has caused in other breeds. Therefore the puppy you acquire is likely to be sound, healthy and typical of its type, both physically and in temperament. Nevertheless, having acquired your puppy you will still need veterinary assistance, even though it may only be for routine inoculations and worming.

FINDING A VETERINARY SURGEON
The choice of your vet is really just as important as the choice of your puppy. If you have never owned a dog before you should know that every breed, even the Bichon Frisé, has its own idiosyncrasies and you will need a veterinary surgeon with some knowledge and rapport with the breed. Remember that a person who may have a reputation for being good with cats, or super with St Bernards, may not necessarily be the ideal vet for toy breeds!

How do you set about choosing your veterinary surgeon? If you have, or have had, other animals or know of a local veterinary surgeon by reputation the task is much easier. Otherwise look in your classified telephone directory, which will at least make you familiar with the names and whereabouts of the local practices.

Don't be afraid to approach people exercising vaguely

similar dogs in your area and enquire where they go for veterinary attention and what they think of the service. I suggest approaching people with Yorkshire Terriers, Poodles, Pekes and other small dogs rather than the owners of large dogs such as Boxers, Borzois or Rottweilers. Very often you will find that one name will crop up more frequently and that is the practice to try first.

Even before you acquire your dog do not be afraid to ring practices and enquire about details of their service. Explain that you are about to acquire a Bichon Frisé and ask them if you are likely to encounter any particular problems. The quality of the reply from the reception staff will at least give you some idea of the service you are likely to receive subsequently.

If you are not impressed, do not be afraid to try elsewhere because the decision you are making is an important one. It is far better to choose carefully before you establish a relationship than to have to change vets at a later stage.

Fees and premises will vary. Do not be impressed too much by either initially. The quality of the service, availability at unsocial hours and willingness to discuss problems are probably more important.

THE FIRST VISIT

Having acquired your puppy from the breeder you will undoubtedly have received instructions about the timing of inoculations and suggestions on when you should visit a veterinary surgeon. This should not be delayed too long after acquiring the puppy so that the vet can check for any hereditary or congenital problems that may have inadvertently escaped the notice of the breeder. However, it is probably a good idea to let the puppy settle down in the new surroundings of your home for a day or two before subjecting it to yet another strange experience! The first visit is often the time for starting vaccination as well as a general health check.

General Health Check

The vet will probably examine the puppy very thoroughly to make sure that you have bought a healthy animal. Don't resent this and please don't be upset if the puppy appears to object to part of the examination. It doesn't understand the reason for it and not surprisingly may object vociferously to the examination, particularly of its private parts!

When vets carry out this examination they are looking for far more than, for example, signs of enteritis or general health. They will examine the skin to make sure there is no eczema, mange or dermatitis present. This will also include a check on the ears. Bichons Frisés as a breed carry a lot of hair around, sometimes in the ear canal, and you may be shown how to remove some of this hair to keep the ear free of obstruction.

The check will include an examination of the bony skeleton. Even in a young puppy abnormalities such as slipping kneecaps can sometimes be revealed which could later lead to lameness. The eyes, nose and mouth will be checked to make sure there are no deformities. A male's testes will be checked to see if they are descended and in the scrotum.

While this examination is proceeding, the vet will probably be asking you questions about feeding and general behaviour. Don't hesitate at this stage to discuss any worries you may have, no matter how trivial you may think them.

A worming programme is also usually suggested at this time. This may be slightly different from the worming routine that has been suggested by the breeder, but do mention any instructions you have been given.

Puppies with Problems

Most Bichon Frisé puppies will pass the health examination without difficulty, but what happens if the veterinary surgeon does find a problem? It may be a physical problem and can be quite minor, for example an abnormality of the bite when the upper and lower jaws do not meet in the correct manner; or there may be joint problems that although minor, could lead to lameness later in life. Temperament problems may sometimes cause the vet concern and need discussion. Any of these problems can be acquired or congenital, that is due to injury or else present from birth.

If the puppy has severe problems the vet may suggest that the puppy is returned to the breeder. This is one of the reasons why it is worthwhile ensuring that your puppy has its first veterinary examination within a short time of buying it. If you don't want to return the puppy, be sure to discuss this with your vet at the time. Remember he or she is working in your best interests. A vet will not be unsympathetic but has a job to do and will carefully explain to you the implications of the problem and then the decision must rest with you.

ROUTINE HEALTH CARE

Having finished the physical examination the vet will discuss feeding, general management, training, worming and vaccination. Remember when you take a puppy to the vet, even just for vaccination, that the cost includes a consultation and that means what it says! Any worries, doubts or problems should be discussed with the vet at this time, no matter how trivial. Don't be shy of making a list of questions you want to ask. Many people feel embarrassed at taking out a list in front of the vet, but don't worry, most vets will be pleased that you've taken the trouble to make one.

If the puppy is a bitch you may want to breed, now is a good time to discuss it, and the problem of heats (oestrus). What are the alternatives? The vet will discuss surgical neutering (spaying) or chemical control with either injection or tablets.

Many novice owners acquire a male puppy and feel they would like to show it and breed from it. This is not quite as easy as it appears at first sight, and the veterinary surgeon will be happy to discuss the various aspects.

VACCINATION

If the puppy is old enough and fit enough vaccination may begin on your first visit. The vaccination programme your vet recommends may well vary from that suggested by the breeder or that of friends with puppies. Vaccination programmes are tailored to the puppy and depend on the incidence of disease in the area, age, breed and other factors.

Most puppies can be vaccinated from about eight weeks old. Canine vaccines usually involve at least two injections, the second one given at around 12 weeks of age. These injections give good protection against the major canine diseases but do remember that no vaccine gives complete protection against any particular disease. However, today's vaccines give a high degree of protection for all the diseases included in the programme.

Inoculation programme

CANINE PARVOVIRUS disease is transmitted by a very resistant virus which can live away from the dog's body for long periods of time. Vaccination gives extremely good protection but it must be boosted annually. Symptoms of the disease are depression, vomiting and diarrhoea, often with blood. Treatment involves intensive care and intravenous fluid therapy and is frequently unsuccessful.

DISTEMPER is the virus disease which, in the 1930s, first led to canine vaccination. Although now less common than in the past it still occurs in epidemic form from time to time. The signs can include vomiting and diarrhoea but usually the animal appears to have a cold, with runny eyes and nose and often a cough. Later nervous signs can develop with twitching and even fits and paralysis.

HARDPAD is a form of distemper which causes hardening of all the pads. The same vaccination gives protection against both distemper and hard pad. Again a yearly booster dose is recommended.

CANINE HEPATITIS is another virus disease against which vaccines give protection. Hepatitis is inflammation of the liver and other internal organs. It is generally referred to as canine adenovirus[1] or CAV[1] disease. Infection is contracted from both faeces and urine and dogs who have recovered from the disease may act as carriers. Signs can include acute hepatitis, hence the original name, but the kidneys are much more commonly affected. The virus can also affect the lungs and cause a respiratory form of the disease but this is more commonly caused by an allied virus, CAV[2], which is part of the kennel cough complex of diseases. Inoculation against CAV[1] and CAV[2] generally provides good protection.

LEPTOSPIROSIS is a bacterial rather than a viral disease but it is incorporated in the canine vaccination programme. Serious illness can result from infection and it can also affect humans. There are two forms in the dog, of which *Leptospira icterohaemorrhagiae* can be passed to humans. The symptoms include fever, jaundice and severe depression. The other form in the dog, *Leptospira canicola*, is also called lamp post disease since it is transmitted by dogs sniffing at one another's urine. The signs are acute kidney problems.

Unlike virus diseases leptospiral diseases can be treated with antibiotics, but prevention is better than cure. Again an annual booster is essential for continuing protection.

INFECTIOUS RHINOTRACHEITIS, the so-called cough syndrome, is popularly known as kennel cough, although it can affect animals that have never been near kennels. It is a highly infectious condition and is caused by a mixture of virus and bacteria. Again, vaccination provides protection. In addition an intranasal vaccine is available in Britain which covers the most important bacterial component of the disease, *Bordatella bronchiseptica*. This vaccine is particularly useful if there is an outbreak of cough in your area or you are about to board your dog. So ask your vet's advice. Bear in mind, however, that this vaccine only provides protection for about six months.

RABIES With strict quarantine laws the UK is rabies free and rabies vaccination is not usually carried out unless the animal is intended for export. In the many countries of the world where rabies occurs puppies need their rabies shots at about the same time as their other inoculations.

COMMON AILMENTS AND DISEASES

Bichons Frisés, although a toy breed, are anything but delicate. They are healthy, hardy little dogs with a long history. Fortunately having not attained the over popularity of some of the other toy breeds they have not suffered the effects of indiscriminate breeding. Let us hope they never will. For this reason they have few problems specific to the breed but they do suffer certain general doggy ailments, the most important of which are described below.

Anal problems

Both dogs and bitches have two small scent glands on either side of the anus. These are normally emptied when the dog defecates. Sometimes, however, things go wrong and they can fill up and cause problems. Signs can vary but excessive licking underneath, biting the tail head, or sometimes scooting or dragging the bottom along the ground are warning signals. Anal sac problems can sometimes be caused by worms, diarrhoea or infection and a visit to the vet is a reasonable precaution. Usually, though, it is just a simple impaction of the glands, in which case the vet may show you how to empty them yourself. Once trouble has started some Bichons Frisés develop a fixation about their anal glands and often bite or chew in the groin or at the base of the tail, particularly when they are under stress. In these cases, if persistent, the vet may advise surgical removal of the glands to provide a permanent solution to the problem and give the pet some peace.

Sometimes, especially in puppies or dogs whose coats have become very overgrown, problems due to faecal mats will be mistaken for anal gland problems. Remember that the standard of the Bichon Frisé states that the coat should fall in soft corkscrew curls. Occasionally if there are too many of these around the anus they get matted with bits of faeces, causing soreness and discomfort, not to mention smell. Careful hygiene is really all that is necessary to prevent or cure this, at the same time ensuring that the hair length, particularly in the adult, does not become excessive around that area.

Bowel problems

Enteritis is every owner's dread, particularly with a puppy, but this is not the only bowel problem.

AN UPSET BOWEL is one of the most common ailments in dogs and the Bichon Frisé is no exception. The most obvious sign of any bowel upset is vomiting and/or diarrhoea. Puppies eat all manner of foreign materials and assault their bowels with foreign bodies such as pebbles, bits of plastic toys etc. which can actually cause a stoppage. Other causes can be infection, poison, parasites, and allergies. A radical change of diet or too many titbits can also upset the bowel's functioning.

First aid for a general bowel upset is relatively simple. Restrict, but do not prevent, fluid intake, since if a dog drinks too much it will bring it back (and often more besides). At the same time, starve the animal for 24 hours and then offer small quantities of light, easily digested food: such as fish, eggs, veal or rabbit. If there is no improvement it should be taken to the vet. If a dog vomits or passes blood the vet should be contacted without delay. An accompanying sample of the faeces is often an aid to diagnosis, especially in the case of puppies.

WIND, FLATUS, OR COLIC is another bowel condition that can affect both the young puppy and, not uncommonly, the elderly dog. Puppies at around weaning will often overeat and become distressed with wind. A good first aid measure is to administer a dose of babies' gripe water or alternatively a preparation containing charcoal. If the puppy is very distressed a visit to the vet is essential.

In the elderly dog the problem is due to the inability of its bowel to contract in a normal manner and so after a meal the poor dog blows up with wind. Again gripe water or a charcoal preparation are good first aid measures. Changing your dog's feeding regime to include more frequent, smaller meals will also do a lot to help. If the condition is severe and the dog in pain, obviously the vet should be contacted.

HAEMORRHAGIC ENTERITIS In many small breeds simple inflammation of the bowel (enteritis), vomiting and diarrhoea can quickly progress to the haemorrhagic form where the poor animal is passing blood at both ends. Canine parvovirus is often the cause of this in puppies but other causes, including toxaemia, shock and infection, can be responsible in adult dogs. *This condition is dangerous and your vet should be contacted without delay.* The animal usually wants to drink copiously but do not allow this because it will only make the condition worse with the dog wanting to vomit ever more frequently. Ice to lick can sometimes help but it is better to give nothing by mouth and to arrange to take the patient to the vet as soon as possible.

Breathing problems

Bichons Frisés are relatively free from breathing problems. However, many have particularly small airways. Any infection resulting in enlargement of the tonsils can cause some breathing problems. The signs are snorting, coughing and respiratory distress. If this occurs a visit to the vet is necessary since a course of antibiotics is usually needed.

Dental problems

DOUBLE DENTITION is a common problem in many of the

miniature breeds but Bichons Frisés appear to suffer less than other toys from this condition. The deciduous, or baby, teeth are not shed when the permanent teeth are fully erupted at about six to nine months old and the dog has a double row of teeth between which food can become lodged and cause infection. If you think your dog has more teeth than it should, consult your vet.

TARTAR AND GUM RECESSION, or calculus and periodontal disease to give them their correct titles, are not uncommon in the Bichon Frisé. The cause is very similar to that in humans. Invisible bacterial plaque is laid down on the teeth resulting in the deposition of tartar, which will cause the gum to recede (periodontal disease) with ultimate loosening of the teeth as the sockets become infected. Today there are specially designed toothbrushes and malt flavoured toothpaste which are worth trying. If you can brush your dog's teeth regularly, it will help prevent tooth loss as well as ensuring that your dog has much sweeter breath and is nice to be near!

In addition regular scaling and polishing will help to preserve your dog's teeth. A dog has to have a general anaesthetic for this to be carried out efficiently.

Ear problems

The breed standard states that the Bichon Frisé's ears should hang close to the head and be well covered with flowing hair. This conformation can lead to lack of ventilation and regular maintenance in the form of grooming and plucking excess hair from the ear canal is necessary (page 75). The lack of ventilation can result in infection in the ear canal, the signs of which are often a brown smelly discharge. If these signs are neglected the condition progresses to soreness of the ear canal and the dog may scratch and cause the whole area to become red and inflamed.

EAR MITES can and do occur particularly when the Bichon Frisé shares a home with cats who carry these tiny mites, often without showing any signs of them. In the dog they can cause intense irritation: scratching and rubbing in turn lead to an inflamed ear canal, excess wax and very soon an infected ear. There are many preparations available from your vet to clear the trouble. Remember that neglected ears can lead to chronic otitis (canker), the cure for which in many cases is fairly extensive and expensive surgery.

Eye problems

The eyes of the Bichon Frisé should be relatively trouble-free from the point of view of conformation—their shape and set. However, the abundance of hair on their faces can lead to irritation of the eyeball and result in chronic conjunctivitis and overflow of tears (epiphora) which in turn causes tear staining on the face. This is always a problem in a white or light-coloured animal. The wetness causes irritation which in turn leads to rubbing and excoriation or ulceration of the face. The condition therefore merits constant attention. Reducing the irritation by trimming the hair does much to resolve the problem.

In some cases the tear ducts may be blocked which results in the tear overflow. In this case seek your vet's help. Treatment for the actual staining of the hair can be difficult. Pet shops stock a multiplicity of remedies, the majority of which are ineffective. If conjunctivitis and infection are both present the tear staining will be worse. In this case antibiotics, sometimes taken over a long period, will improve matters. In any case discuss the matter with your vet before trying any of the over-the-counter remedies.

Fits and collapse

A dog in a fit is unconscious and not aware of what is happening. Onlookers certainly are and very frightening it can be. Fits occur for many reasons and generally last only a few seconds, during which a dog may urinate and defecate. When the dog comes out of the fit it can neither see nor hear properly for a short while and so may even bite its owner in self-defence.

Fits in puppies can be due to infections such as distemper, as well as worms, colic and many other causes.

Collapse is very uncommon in the Bichon Frisé but can occur in the older dog due to defective circulation or heart problems.

Heart diseases

These are relatively infrequent in the breed except in the older obese animal when the first sign is often a chronic cough, particularly when the dog becomes excited, and first gets up from rest.

Hip problems

Many of the toy breeds suffer from problems involving the hip joint. Von Perthes disease, an enlargement and degeneration of the head of the femur, occurs at around five months of age just before the puppy is full grown and is due to failure of the blood supply to the hip during the growth period. Corrective surgery is usually extremely successful.

Lameness

Slipping kneecaps, slipping stifle, or more correctly luxation of the patellae, is not unknown in the Bichon Frisé and often results in the intermittent lifting of one or both hindlegs when walking or running. It can be due to an injury such as a strain, but is more likely to be of congenital origin. Although any hereditary implications have not been fully worked out it is obviously sensible not to breed from affected animals.

With modern veterinary orthopaedic surgery correction of the condition even in very young animals can be remarkably successful.

Obesity

Fatness should not be a problem if your dog is correctly fed and not over-indulged. However, many middle-aged Bichons Frisés do seem to become overweight. This is usually due to over-indulgence with the wrong foods. Do take your vet's advice and do not be afraid of consulting him or her if you think your dog is getting a little plump. Bichons Frisés do have a long coat and this often disguises increasing girth. A weight check is the most sensible way of keeping tabs on obesity. Weigh yourself on the bathroom scales and then yourself plus dog. Do this regularly, perhaps monthly, so any increase in the dog's weight is quickly apparent and appropriate action can be taken.

Remember that obesity can lead to breathing and heart disease but probably more commonly to joint problems and lameness. As a first aid measure reduce all titbits and starchy and fatty foods.

Skin problems

Bichons Frisés like other white dogs can frequently have sensitive skins. Much can be done to prevent a chronic condition developing.

ALLERGIC SKIN CONDITIONS Contact allergies can develop due to sensitivity to plants, carpets, man-made car seat covers and other materials and objects with which your dog may come in contact. The irritation is usually on the more hairless parts of the skin, the feet and underparts and will frequently need sustained treatment to effect a cure.

ATOPY is an inhalation allergy, rather like hayfever and asthma in humans. In the dog inhaled pollens can cause itching round the face and feet and other parts of the skin. Allergies caused by particular foods can occur, but these are rare.

All these allergic skin problems need veterinary help. The results can be a localised or generalised eczema (dermatitis or inflammation of the skin) which causes the dog great discomfort. Although local application of antihistamine creams and lotions containing calamine will bring temporary relief the underlying cause will need to be determined.

PARASITIC SKIN PROBLEMS Fleas and lice can also cause irritation and result in patches of eczema. Puppies should be regularly checked for fleas and lice and one of the various effective sprays or baths obtainable from your vet used regularly. Remember that fleas, unlike lice, breed away from the body and therefore the environment also has to be treated. Again your vet will recommend the appropriate products.

MANGE is not a great problem in the breed, unlike some other toy breeds, but it can occur. There are two forms, both due to tiny mites that burrow in the layers of the skin. Sarcoptic mange can cause scabies in humans and causes intense irritation both in the dog and infected owner. Demodectic mange sometimes results in hairless patches without very much irritation and is due to a mite that lives deep in the hair follicles.

Diagnosis of either form of mange depends on skin scrapings and once diagnosed the condition can be treated accordingly. Early consultation with your vet is essential in the case of any skin problem.

Travel sickness

Puppies and dogs of many breeds, not least among them the Bichon Frisé, can suffer from travel or motion sickness and vets are frequently consulted about this problem. Many cases can be overcome by careful training.

You should start the puppy travelling young, holding it and distracting its attention from the vehicle movement, ensuring you are well supplied with towels and covering your clothes with polythene. This may do the trick! Ensure the journeys are very short. Alternatively transport the puppy in a cardboard box so that it cannot see out through the windows and be upset by passing objects and the sensation of movement. Gradually increase the length of the journeys.

If you are not successful try one of the human travel sickness remedies. Most Bichon Frisé puppies require about half a tablet. There are various makes on the market available without prescription. They have different formulations and before consulting the vet it may be worthwhile trying different brands to see if one is effective. If you have to depend on tablets prescribed by the vet you will always have to ensure that you have them with you and have an adequate supply.

Worms

ROUNDWORMS can be particularly bothersome in puppies. They can be infested from their mothers before they are born and be passing worm eggs out in their faeces by the time they are 11 days old. Frequently evidence of the worms themselves is not apparent unless the puppy is ill and vomits. However, your vet can detect their presence by a simple faecal test and may request a sample of the puppy's stool. In any case puppies should be regularly wormed every four weeks until they are about six months old, particularly for roundworms, although occasionally tapeworms will affect the young animal.

From six months onwards, worming with a preparation that covers roundworm, tapeworm and the other types of worm makes good sense; your vet will advise you. Today there are very safe and very effective remedies on the market which involve no inconvenience to the owner or the animal, but it is always worth seeking veterinary advice before buying any remedies over the counter.

TAPEWORMS, unlike roundworms, cannot be passed directly from dog to dog but must pass through an intermediate host. The most common urban tapeworm, *Dipylidium caninum*, has the flea as an intermediate host. In country areas, where there are more varieties of animal than in a town, a dog can be infested with different types of tapeworm. Regular deworming removes any danger to the dog.

PET HEALTH INSURANCE
Several excellent pet health insurance schemes are available today, particularly those from specialist companies. These policies, although not covering routine vaccination, worming, whelping and dental treatment, certainly cover all unexpected veterinary bills as well as chronic conditions up to the insured limit for any one condition.

Veterinary expertise is rapidly expanding and conditions that were untreatable a few years ago are now regularly and routinely treated. Cancer is only one example of this. The expertise and care necessary for effecting these cures has to be paid for and unfortunately veterinary fees are increasing. Talk to your vet about pet health insurance.

Appendix 1
UK Champions

Championship status was granted to the Bichon Frisé for the first time in 1980; at that time the Kennel Club registrations for the breed stood at 477. Six sets of Challenge Certificates were allocated, these were on offer at the four representative Championship Shows: Crufts, judge Mr Lionel Hamilton Renwick; Birmingham Dog Show Society, judge Mr Andrew Brace; Scottish Kennel Club, judge Mrs Wendy Streatfield and the Welsh Kennel Club, judge Mrs Muriel Lewin. The two others were the United Kingdom Toy Dog Society, judge Mr Terry Thorn, and Driffield Agricultural Society, judge Mr Graham Newell. From these first shows in 1980 two champions emerged Ch Gosmore Tresilva Zorba and Ch Glenfolly Silver Lady of Sarabande. These two were the first English Champions in the history of the breed.

The Kennel Club registrations for the year ending 1988 were 1021 and in 1989 26 sets of Challenge Certificates were allocated to the Bichon Frisé.

List of all UK Champions

1980 Ch Gosmore Tresilva Zorba D 15.9.77
      Breeder/Owner Mrs J Ransom
      Sire Zethus de Chaponay of Tresilva *Dam* Tresilva Aura

      Ch Glenfolly Silver Lady of Sarabande B 14.2.77
      Breeder Mrs C Coley *Owner* Mrs A Worth
      Sire Leander Beaumonde Snow Puff *Dam* Carlise Colombine

1981   Ch Montravia Persan Make Mine Mink D 20.3.79
Breeder Mrs P Perry *Owner* Mrs P Gibbs
Sire Int Ch If de la Buthiere of Antarctica
Dam Leander Pleasures Persan.

Ch Montravia Snow Dream B 24.2.79
Breeder/Owner Mrs P Gibbs
Sire Montravia Leander Snow Fox *Dam* Montravia
Leander Snow Princess

1982   Ch Cluneen Jolly Jason of Hunkidori D 25.5.77
Breeder Mrs E Banks *Owner* Mrs J Fender
Sire Cluneen Lejerdell Silver Starshine *Dam* Cluneen
Lejerdell Tarzanna

Ch Leijazulip Kipling of Shamaney D 10.9.78 (**p. 82**)
Breeder D. Chiverton & Mrs V Goold *Owner* Miss
M Flintoft
Sire Leijazulip Guillaume *Dam* Ninon de la Buthiere
of Leijazulip

Ch Persan Top Button B 10.3.78
Breeders/Owners Mr & Mrs Perry
Sire Am Ch Vogelflights Choir Boy of Leander
Dam Leander Dora of Persan

Ch Leijazulip Jazz of Zudiki D 18.3.81
Breeder D. Chiverton & Mrs V Goold *Owner* Mrs J
Brown
Sire Leijazulip Guillaume *Dam* Ninon de la Buthiere
of Leijazulip

Ch Efaldees Angelic Faith B 5.3.80
Breeder/Owner Mr & Mrs A Buxton
Sire Leander Beaumonde Snow Puff *Dam* Huntglen
Zarah de Chaponay at Efaldees

Ch Gosmore Tresilva Zorba

Ch Glenfolly Silver Lady of Sarabande

Ch Montravia Snow Dream

Ch Cluneen Jolly Jason of Hunkidori

Ch Leijazulip Jazz of Zudiki

Ch Snarsnoz Dancing Rhythm at Melsel

Ch Rossage Royal Snow Queen at Maybeth

Ch Caywood Little Jack Horner

Ch Jaqueline of Leijazulip at Tresilva

1983   Ch Snarsnoz Show Quest at Melsel D 23.1.81
Breeder Mrs R Seaman *Owner* Mrs C Belcher
Sire Hunkidori Bobbi Shafto *Dam* Chitinas Tudor
Melody

Ch Snarsnoz Dancing Rhythm at Melsel B 31.3.80
Breeder Mrs R Seaman *Owner* Mrs C Belcher
Sire Hunkidori Bobbi Shafto *Dam* Chitinas Tudor
Melody

Ch Rossage Royal Snow Queen at Maybeth B 9.12.79
Breeder/Owner Mrs B Satchell
Sire Leander Beaumonde Snow Puff *Dam* Barryville
Little Mitzi

Ch Kynismar Black Eyed Susie B 19.8.81
Breeder/Owner Mrs M Atkins
Sire Kingarth Dapper Dan at Kynismar *Dam* Persan
Madam

1984   Ch Caywood Little Jack Horner D 19.12.80
Breeder Mrs S Baker *Owner* Mr & Mrs G Armstrong
Sire Am Ch C & D's Prince Charles at Caywood
Dam Devon's Heavens to Betsy

Eng & Ir Ch Sulyka Snoopy D 25.2.82 9 **opp. p. 97**)
Breeder/Owner Mrs S Dunger
Sire Ch Leijazulip Jazz of Zudiki *Dam* Shamaney My
Choice of Sulyka

Ch Jaqueline of Leijazulip at Tresilva B 26.7.82
Breeder Mrs Bendall *Owner* Mrs J Ransom
Sire Leijazulip Benji *Dam* Tresilva Marianne

Ch Leander the Sundancer B 29.1.82
Breeder/Owner Mrs W Streatfield & Ms S Wheeler
Sire Snow Dog of Leander *Dam* Leander Snow Chime

Ch Sibon Jasmyn B 10.8.83
Breeder/Owner Mrs M Binder
Sire Ch Leijazulip Kipling of Shamaney *Dam* Sibon
Soda Pop

1985 Eng & Ir Ch Tiopepi Mad Louie at Pamplona
D 13.9.82   **(p. 81)**
Breeder Mrs C Coxall *Owner* Mr M Coad
Sire Ch Montravia Persan Make Mine Mink
Dam Leijazulip Sabina of Colhamdorn

Ch Hunkidori Personality Miss B 18.4.82
Breeder Mr & Mrs Fender *Owner* Mrs Fender & Mr
Woodward
Sire Ch Leijazulip Jazz of Zudiki *Dam* Cluneen
Happi Heidi of Hunkidori

Ch Pengorse Felicity of Tresilva B. 21.6.83 **(opp. p.32)**
Breeder Mrs Bendall *Owner* Miss M Ransom
Sire Leijazulip Gioberti *Dam* Tresilva Marianne

1986 Ch Kynismar Black Eyed Boogaloo D 10.2.85 **(p. 68)**
Breeder/Owner Mrs M Atkins
Sire Shamaney Stepping Out at Kynismar *Dam* Ch
Kynismar Black Eyed Susie

Ch Simway Shantung B 12.5.83
Breeder/Owner Mr & Mrs I Farmer
Sire Ligray Sweet Alysum *Dam* Marydale's Just Fancy
at Simway

Ch Melsel Cracklin Rosie B 24.6.84
Breeder/Owner Mr R Blackwell & Mrs C Belcher
Sire Ch Snarsnoz Show Quest at Melsel *Dam* Kynis-
mar Spandau Ballet

Ch Rossage Silver Locket B 14.1.84
Breeder/Owner Mrs B Satchell
Sire Rossage Snow Drift *Dam* Ch Rossage Royal Snow
Queen at Maybeth

Top *Ch Sibon Jasmyn*
Above left *Ch Simway Shan-*
tung
Above right *Ch Melsel Crack-*
lin Rosie
Left *Ch Bumbleridge Overture*
at Rossage

Ch Edelweiss Ebony Eyes

Ch Emmrill Snow Pipit

Ch Roushka's Song and Dance

Ch Bobander Toot the Flute

Ch Roushka's Dancemaster

Ch Bumbleridge Overture at Rossage
B 25.10.84   (p. 121)
Breeder Mrs C Nicholls *Owner* Mrs B Satchell
Sire Rossage Snow Drift *Dam* Ligray Tyoo-Tyoo at
Bumbleridge

1987   Ch Edelweiss Ebony Eyes D 18.1.84
Breeder Miss S Beeston *Owner* Mrs E Beeston
Sire Am Ch C & D's Prince Charles of Caywood
Dam Cascadia Cinzano

Ch Emmrill Snow Pipit D 18.4.84
Breeder Mrs M Huxham *Owner* Mr & Mrs H Frith
Sire Eng & Ir Ch Sulyka Snoopy *Dam* Twinley
Princess Flavia

Ch Roushka's Song and Dance B 30.1.85
Breeder Mr D Thomas *Owner* Mr S Thompson
Sire Ch Leijazulip Kipling of Shamaney *Dam* Bwena-
mor Christmas Cracker of Montravia

Ch Bobander Toot the Flute B 27.5.85
Breeder/Owner Mrs C Wyatt
Sire Eng & Ir Ch Sulyka Snoopy *Dam* Shamaney
Manhatten of Bobander

1988   Ch Kynismar Boogies Boy D 29.4.86
Breeder/Owner Mrs M Atkins
Sire Ch Kynismar Black Eyed Boogaloo *Dam* Kynis-
mar Campanula

Ch Roushka's Dancemaster D 20.7.84
Breeder/Owner Mr D Thomas
Sire Ch Leijazulip Kipling of Shamaney *Dam* Bwena-
mor Christmas Cracker

Ch Ligray Smartypants at Ricanna D 4.12.86
Breeder Mrs D Jones *Owner* Mrs A Stafferton
Sire Ligray Precious Gift *Dam* Ligray Uptown Girl

Ch Ligray Mr Beau Geste D 31.12.82
Breeder Mr G & Mrs E Fellowes *Owner* Mr B Diaper
Sire Am Ch C & D's Starmaker of Leander
Dam Pyrhaven Amour

Ch Sibon Sloane Ranger at Pamplona D 12.9.86
Breeder Mrs M Binder *Owner* Mr M Coad & Mrs J
Cohen
Sire Eng & Ir Ch Tiopepi Mad Louie at Pamplona
Dam Ch Sibon Jasmyn

Ch Melsel Kiss Me Kate B 2.5.85
Breeder Mrs C Belcher *Owner* Mrs L Gisborne
Sire Kynismar Mystic Magic at Melsel
Dam Ch Snarsnoz Dancing Rhythm at Melsel

Ch Kynismar Heaven Sent to Roushka B 25.12.86
Breeder/Owner Mrs M Atkins
Sire Ch Kynismar Black Eyed Boogaloo *Dam* Kynismar Campanula

1989   Ch Rusmar Xmas Magic D 25.12.86
Breeder/Owner Mrs D Russell
Sire Ch Kynismar Black Eyed Boogaloo *Dam* Rusmar
Sea Angel of Zudiki

Ch Sulyka Puzzle D 24.8.87
Breeder/Owner Mrs S Dunger
Sire Puffin Billy of Sulyka *Dam* Fascination of Zudiki
at Sulyka

Ch Ligray Mr Beau Geste

Ch Sibon Sloane Ranger at Pamplona

Ch Melsel Kiss Me Kate

Ch Kynismar Heaven Sent to Roushka

Ch Rusmar Xmas Magic

Ch Sulyka Puzzle

Ch Kynismar Billy the Kid

Ch Orpheus Orion of Atroya

Ch Kynismar Billy the Kid D 15.11.86
Breeder/Owner Mrs M Atkins
Sire Ch Kynismar Black Eyed Boogaloo *Dam* Kynismar Take a Chance on Me

Ch Rossage Silver Ghost D 10.5.87
Breeder/Owner Mrs B Satchell
Sire Eng & Ir Ch Tiopepi Mad Louie at Pamplona
Dam Ch Rossage Silver Locket

Ch Orpheus Orion of Atroya D 7.1.86
Breeder Mrs S Bignell *Owner* Mr & Mrs A Banfield
Sire Pengorse Poldark of Tresilva *Dam* Dolly Day Dream

Ch Leander Snow Cat B 26.6.85
Breeder/Owner Mrs W Streatfield and Ms S Wheeler
Sire Am Ch C & D's Starmaker of Leander
Dam Leander White Lace

Ch Sibon Fatal Attraction at Pamplona
B 25.2.88 (opp. p. 65)
Breeder Mrs M Binder *Owner* Mr M Coad
Sire Pengorse Poldark of Tresilva *Dam* Ch Sibon Jasmyn

Ch Leander Snow Cat   *Ch Rossage Silver Ghost*

Appendix 2
Breed Affixes

ALAREEN	Mr & Mrs A Miles	BRADEL	Mr & Mrs E Bradley
ALASHIR	Mrs S Preston	BRETARAH	Mrs E L Allen
ALBANEY	Mrs J Jensen	BROOKLEES	Mr & Mrs T J Brookes
ALLSLEE	Mrs F M Taylor	BUMBLERIDGE	Mr & Mrs C G Nicholls
ALONDO	Mrs R Gamgee	BUZANDO	Mrs J Earland
ALOST	Mr & Mrs L J & J R Hoebeeck	BWENAMOR	Mrs S Ruiz
ALTOVIV	Mrs V A Kelly	BYLENA	Mrs L Martindale
AMERTAIN	Mrs G J Burchfield	CALGREA	Mrs C A Hopper
ANDANTINOS	Msdms B McManus & K Jeskins	CAMBOALTO	Mr W Ogilvie
ANTARCTICA	Mr & the late Mrs K B Rawlings	CARLORIAN	Mrs M Nunn
ANTONSHILL	Mr & Mrs W & E Gray	CARRYMERS	Mr & Mrs McKenna
ANTRIX	Mrs A Kennedy	CASAROW	Mr C Sparrow
APPLEACRE	Mrs P Holbrook O'Hara	CASCADIA	Mrs S A Pudney
ARAZELLE	Miss D D Nelson	CASSAWAKE	Mrs R Cass
ARKANGEL	Mr & Mrs T & M Holder	CASTLEGARNSTONE	Mrs V J O'Keeffe
ASILENE	Mrs E Beeston	CAYWOOD	Miss S H Baker
ATASTAR	Mr P Langdon	CEROMA	Mrs O Pinches
ATROYA	Mr & Mrs A R Banfield	CHALEBAY	Mrs L Sprake
AUFRAISE	Mrs C L O'Neill	CHANSARY	Mrs S A Edwards
AVANA	Miss J Smith	CHARWICOT	Miss V Hiller
AZZJAZZ	Mr & Mrs G & M Adams	CHRISTARICK	Mrs C J Eagle
BABAJEN	Mrs B Kidsley & Miss J A Wells	CLANMARRET	Mr & Mrs T & M E Holgate
BALNEATH	Mrs V Giles	CLUNEEN	Mrs E Banks
BAMFYLDE	Mr & Mrs C R Webb	COELEGANT	Mrs J O Falconer-Atlee
BARDELIN	Miss B Lasenby	COLLENCO	Miss C Gittins
BARKLOTS	Mr T D Mather	COPACABANA	Miss S G Falkingham
BEAUMONDE	Mr R G Beaumonde, Mr D Thomas & Mr & Mrs A G Mills	CYANDRA	Mr C & Mrs S Neale
		DAISYBANK	Mrs J Daws
BAUPRES	The late Mrs E & Miss F Mirylees	DALGIG	Mrs S Smith
BECHLA	Mrs P B Hudson	DASHIRS	Mr & Mrs D J & S E M Miles
BECKVILLA	Mrs M Beck	DAVYLUVS	Mr D Black
BELLETOILE	Mrs P A Ward-Davey	DEBATHE	Mr & Mrs D E & A W Holmes
BENANN	Mr F B & Mr A M D Davies	DEBERON	Mr & Mrs R A & D W Smith
BESBARDA	Mrs B Johnson	DEELVAS	Mr J & Mrs D Lee
BIBICHE	Mrs J Bosson	DENINOR	Mr D A & Mrs N A Higlett
BICHAE	Mr & Mrs Etienne	DINORK	Mrs & Miss S & C Myclark
BLANCHARD	Mrs A Stelling	DOKHAM	Mr G P Newell
BOBANDER	Mrs C Wyatt	DRAKESLEAT	Mrs Z Thorn-Andrews
BOCHIN	Mrs C Alcock	DRUIDCROWN	Mr & Mrs W F & B M Markham
BOREALIS	Mrs E K Scott	DRUIDSWOOD	Mesdames M Pickup & D Tustian
BOXATRIX	Mrs P M Hardcastle		Mrs M Pickup
BRACKENDYNE	Mesdames J Fossett & E Bracken	DUKELLE	Mr & Mrs R A Jackson

DUPRE	Mrs J Leonard	KEIDA	Mrs D A Damsell
EDENCOTE	Mr & Mrs C F Bevis	KEMOSA	Mr N & Mrs S Armstrong-Moakes
EDGELMCLERE	Mrs E E Garrett	KERISMICS	Mr & Mrs M J & C A Gunn
EFALDEES	Mr & Mrs A W Buxton	KESDALE	Mrs J L P McIntosh
ELANDMEAD	Mrs J Fagan	KINGARTH	Mrs I M Andree
ELLWIN	Mrs M E Lewin	KRASNA	Mrs D M Kaprockyj
ELZANES	Mr T E Bromell	KYNISMAR	Mrs M F Atkins
EMMRILL	Mrs M G Huxham	LADYHAY	Mr & Mrs N G Hurst
ENCHANTYA	Mrs L Drackford	LAMEDA	Messrs J P Smith & G Carter
ESTIRIS	Mr P King	LANGUILLA	Mesdames L Macleod & M P Hill
FANROY	Mr & Mrs R Forster		Mrs L Macleod
FANTASQUE	Mr C N & Mrs V J Baylis		Mrs M P Hill
FIDELIS	Mr & Mrs R W L & J K Martin	LAPIPKA	Mr & Mrs H M R & J E A Frith
FOELFEDW	Mrs M J Howells	LAUBERTON	Messrs L & A Digby & Mrs Digby
FOUGERE	Mr & Mrs N J Stapley	LEANDER	Mrs W Streatfield/Ms M Wheeler
FRENABRI	Mrs D L Leeks	LEETUNG	Mr & Mrs J & M Evans
FRENDORS	Mrs D Harvey	LEIGHAM	Mrs S Nelson
GERRYDEANS	Mrs D Smith	LEIJAZULIP	Mrs V Goold & Mr D Chiverton
GESBOB	Mrs G Maunder	LIGRAY	Mr & Mrs G & E Fellowes
GILAUNDA	Mrs G M Saunders	LIMARNA	Mrs A Dean
GLAMANTA	Mr & Mrs M Howe	LINSGALE	Miss G M Riley
GLENFLEUR	Mrs E J McConkey	LITTLECOURT	Mrs F Mcgregor
GLENFOLLY	Mrs C M Coley	LOUISIANNA	Miss L Jones
GOSMORE	Mrs A Dallison	LYNBYL	Mr & Mrs W Thomson
GRANASIL	Mr & Mrs J Grant	LYNELBA	Mr B D & Mrs L Gisborne
GRIMMA	Mrs I M Bushell	MAGGANDIE	Mr & Mrs D J & M M E Message
GYLLIS	Mrs G Connell	MAHENDI	Mrs M Hoad
HARENE	Mrs I Ellis	MALACARNE	Mrs D R Twell
HAVENBOROUGH	Mr H D & Mrs J A Rommell	MANDRIA	Mrs H B Gore
HICKER	Mr S & Mrs M Hicks	MANIAN	Mr & Mrs M C W Price
HIELYGHS	Mrs B P Aldridge	MANORBRAE	Miss J A Coats
HIGHAUDAN	Mrs A & Miss S Bacon	MARBELLA	Mrs B Bell
HIGHWORTH	Mrs E A Ashworth	MARTRE	Mr T E & Mrs M M Roberts
HONEYLYN	Mr & Mrs G & B Ellis	MARYDALE	Mrs M Hayward
HUNKIDORI	Mrs J Fender	MAYENA	Mrs M Holmes
HUNTGLEN	Mrs M V Harper	MELSEL	Mr R Blackwell & Mrs C Belcher
HYDEALS	Mrs H Candlin		Mrs C L Belcher
HYLACER	Mr & Mrs L V & B Dickinson	MERRITAYL	Mrs V A Taylor
IADORE	Miss D S Poulter	MEVILLE	Mrs H Davidson
ILCIA	Mrs D M A Simmons	MONTRAVIA	Mrs P Gibbs
ISTONES	Mrs H Tytler	MORDONNOW	Mrs M V Farmer
JANGERRA	Mrs J D R Gray	MOYNA	Mrs B Birch
JANPAL	Mrs & Miss J & J Calderwood	MULBURY	Mrs C Y M Mullen
JARANDA	Mrs J A Buck	MUSKELLA	Mrs B K Mitchell
JASC	Mrs J E Garbutt	MUSONERI	Mrs R M Maher
JAYLEA	Mrs J P Sandford	MYOSOTIS	Mrs M A Watson
JEMAPHIA	Mrs P A Davis	MYRGWYN	Mr & Mrs G & M J Rees
JENTONA	Mrs J E Newman	NAEJEKIM	Mr M W & Mrs J P Bebbington
JOANDRA	Mrs S U Baldwin	NAGAZUMI	Mrs S B Collyer
JOGELA	Mrs A M Baxter	NERAM	Mr & Mrs K & M Pascoe-Price
JONAMARA	Dr W P Jones-Key	NEVILLESON	Mrs E N Neville
JOSANCO	Miss J A Frow	NORJONS	Mrs L D Mitchell
JUBAL	Mr M J & Mrs P A Buckle	NORTONCHASE	Mr & Mrs V C & V E Perfit
JUDAMIE	Mrs J M Lloyd	ORAMSARBOUR	Mrs C Holmes
JUSKALME	Mrs M P Hill	ORCHIDANEGRA	Mrs S Hills
KAYALAN	Mr A Crossley	ORKYARD	Mr & Mrs D R & J Schofield

PADWORTH	Mrs P E Prestidge	SPELGA	Mr & Mrs J G Keery
PAMPLONA	Mr M Coad	STARCOURT	Mrs S D Alexander
PANDEMOS	Miss E R Cormack	STARFORTH	Mr M J Beater
PANICH	Mrs P A Clarke	STEVO	Mr S Thompson
PENGORSE	Mrs M Bendall	STRASSA	Miss J Blunden
PENLUM	Messrs Lumsden & Pennington	STRYDONIA	Mrs D Story
PENWYVERN	Mr & Mrs P J & S A Cole	SUANALV	Mrs J Davies
PERSAN	Mr & Mrs P Perry	SUBOO	Mrs J Morton
PHIEOS	Mrs J Broadhurst	SULYKA	Mrs S M Dunger
PHILBO	Mrs P Houston	SUPERCHERI	Miss C Robilliard
POMANNA	Mrs M E Welsby	TALEECA	Mrs M A Catley
POMLYN	Mrs S L Webster	TAMALVA	Mrs V J Cumpstey
PROPERANSUM	Mr K R & Mrs C A Lampier	TANGLEDWEBB	Mrs P Douglas
PYRILLON	Mr & Mrs C T Bowker	TENERIVA	Mrs W Moore
RALBENIC	Mrs M E Cawdron	TERACITA	Mrs C S Kaye
RETA	Mrs S C Whitelock	THISTLEBECK	Mrs M Y Dobson
RICANNA	Mrs A Stafferton	TIADAWNI	Mrs J Edwards
RIGNOLLA	Mrs N D Rignall	TIARIAN	Mr & Mrs A Richardson
RIORDAN	Mr N J Skeet	TIBAPOLIZA	Mrs J B Ewer
RIVA	Mrs J Kilgour-Smith	TIKISMAS	Mrs K A Robinson
ROCKMEAD	Mrs M A Rabson	TILLDAWN	Mrs I Pinfield
ROHENE	Mrs D Jolly	TIOPEPI	Mrs C E Coxall
ROSICA	Mrs B V Lewis	TOOMAI	Mrs J G Wardle
ROSSAGE	Mrs B Satchell	TOYJOY	Mrs S Goligher
ROSYLE	Mrs S Wright	TRECARNE	Mrs G Ashby
ROUSHKA	Mr D Thomas	TRESILVA	Mrs E J Ransom
ROXARA	Mrs A E Halliwell	TRIBLEN	Mrs E Flanagan
ROYELLA	Mrs G A Taylor	TUDORGABLES	Mrs Beattie
RUPALI	Mrs M J Datta	TUMLADEN	Mrs D J Williams
RUSMAR	Mrs D Russell	TWELVESROW	Mr & Mrs R Carter
SAKOMI	Mesdames J Milner & T A Bastow	TWINLEY	Mrs P B Block
SAMOTO	Mrs I Watson	VESSONGS	Mr & Mrs R E & P M Richardson
SANDPA	Mrs S Holmes	VYTHEA	Mrs A M Pleasants
SANIBEL	Mrs M Lane		Mrs I Colvin
SARABANDE	Mr & Mrs N A Worth	WALDERBRET	Mr & Mrs G W Edwards
SARGETA	Mrs K Page	WALNEL	Mr W Berry D F M
SCOSHA	Mrs E McLaren	WARMINGHAM	Mrs A Lee
SEAHART	Mrs V Campbell	WATTWAY	Miss M H Way
SHALMA	Mr M P J & Mrs S A Marshall	WELLSTREE	Mr D K & Mrs A S Chisholm
SHAMANEY	Mrs M Flintoft-Black	WENTRES	Miss W Greves
SHARBONNE	Miss Y Border		Mrs M Greves
SHAWHILLS	Mrs M Roberts	WILLOWHIP	Mrs E Veal
SHIMERONE	Mrs P M Price	WISHART	Miss D Cormack
SHIRALOU	Mr R A L Harris	WOLSE	Mr & Mrs D & F Ring
SHOLEEN	Mrs E D Spavin & Miss S D Grieve	WYBNELLA	Mrs W Allenby
SCHOOLTERS	Mrs E Jack	ZAPENNE	Mr & Mrs P Bryant
SHOREMEL	Mrs J M Rose	ZARMINE	Mrs M R Booth
SHORNOEL	Mr C G & Mrs R Cundall	ZENYATTA	Mrs C Farmer
SIBON	Mrs M Binder	ZILKEN	Mr K A & Mrs E Sayer
SILVERELVES	Mrs J H F Milne	ZLUDA	Mrs T Zendel
SIMWAY	Mr & Mrs I Farmer	ZUDIKI	Mrs J Brown-Emmerson
SMITHSACRE	Mrs J Smith	ZYKHARA	Mr & Mrs B Corney
SNARSNOZ	Mr & Mrs C W Seaman		

Kennel Club Registrations for the Bichon Frisé
1973 to June 1989

1973	Nil
1974	6
1975	27
1976	31
1977	107
1978	211
1979	354
1980	477
1981	387
1982	520
1983	603
1984	738
1985	794
1986	864
1987	1055
1988	1021
1989	1903

The Bichon Frisé has the fifth highest registration in the Toy Group in Britain.

Appendix 4
Pedigrees of general interest

First USA import
EDDY WHITE DE STEREN VOR (D: Born 1955 France)

Int Ch Bandit de Steren
  Vor

    Amy de Merleroux

    Aress de Steren Vor

    Uistiti

Ami du Lary

    Wallys

Pedigrees of first imports from USA
CLUNEEN LEJERDELL'S TARZANNA (B: Born 3 June 1973)
Breeders: Jerome & Debra Podell, USA. Imported by
  Mrs E Banks February 1974

Int Ch Tarzan de la
  Persaliere 2 June 1970

    Quillan of Milton

      Isico of Milton

      Maya of Milton

    Maya of Milton

      Kwiki of Milton

      Giselle of Milton

Teneriffa de la Persaliere

    Marouf of Milton

      Kito of Milton

      Giselle of Milton

    Quincey of Milton

      Kito of Milton

      Giselle of Milton

CLUNEEN LEJERDELL SILVER STARSHINE (D: Born 29
November 1973)
Breeders: E. Wall & J. Podell, USA. Imported by Mrs E. Banks
1975

		Rank's Esprit du Lejerdell
	Lejerdell's Polar Bear	
Lejerdell's Cub de Bear		Snow White de Villa Sainval
		Ch Cali-Col's Octavius Caesar
	Braymars Lady Juliet	
		Reenroy's Raie du Clair
		Dual In Ch Tarzan de la Persaliere
	Am Ch Lejedell's Leo D Lion of Rank	
Rank's Sassy Lady du Lejerdell		Teneriffa de la Persaliere
		Ch Stardom's Odin Rex Jr
	Rank's Rene	
		Stardom's Summer Snow

Am Ch BEAUMONDE THE SNOWDRIFT OF LEANDER
(D: Born 2 January 1975)
Breeders, Mr R. Beauchamp & Mrs J. Ellis, USA. Imported by
Mr & Mrs J. Streatfield 1975

		Mex Ch Dapper Dan de Gascoigne
	Am Ch Cali-Col's Robespierre	
Am Ch Chaminade Mr Beau Monde		Lyne of Milton
		Mex Ch Dapper Dan de Gascoigne
	Am Ch Reenroy's Ami du Kilkanny	
		Little Nell of Cali-Col
		Monsieur Mieux
	Petit Galant de St George	
Am Ch Works D'Artes a Chaminade		Cali-Col's Nugget
		Mex Ch Dapper Dan de Gascoigne
	Am Ch Cali-Col's Candida	
		Lyne of Milton

Am Ch BEAU MONDE THE DOVE OF LEANDER (B: Born 10 December 1974)

Breeders: R. Beauchamp & P. Waterman, USA. Imported by Mr & Mrs J. Streatfield 1975

Am Int Ch C & D's Count Kristopher	Peppe de Barnette	Quintal de Wanarbry
		Romance de Bourbriel
	Quentia of Goldysdale	Ombre de la Roche Posay
		Oree de la Roche Posay
Am Ch Beau Monde The Vamp	Am Ch Chaminade Mr Beau Monde	Ch Cali-Col's Robespierre
		Ch Reenroy's Ami du Kilkanny
	EE's R Royale Trinquette	Petit Galant de St George
		EE's R Cali-Col's Ritzy Ruffles

Am Ch VOGELFLIGHT'S CHOIR BOY OF LEANDER (D: Born 19 February 1975)

Breeder: M. Vogel, USA. Imported by Mrs W. Streatfield 1976

Am Ch Chaminade Mr Beau Monde	Cali-Col's Robespierre	Mex Ch Dapper Dan de Gascoigne
		Lyne of Milton
	Reenroy's Ami Du Kilkanny	Mex Ch Dapper Dan de Gascoigne
		Little Nell of Cali-Col
Am Ch Vogelflight's Diandee Amy Pouf	C & D's Ch Teeny Tepee's Cherokee Prince	Reenroy's Regal Beau
		Teeny Tepee's Mauri Juleene
	Vogelflight's Diandee Pouf	Tinker II of Rich-Lo
		Vogelflight's Be Be Zwingalee

INT CH XORBA DE CHAPONAY (D: Born 24 September 1973)
Breeders: Mr & Mrs Vansteenkiste-Deleu, Belgium

Ugo de Villa Sainval	Int Ch Racha de Villa Sainval	Kwiki of Milton
		Mowglia of Milton
	Soraya de Villa Sainval	Quillan of Milton
		Mowglia of Milton
Quatna of Milton	Kito of Milton	Abelli of Milton
		Giselle of Milton
	Giselle of Milton	Ch (1951) Youbi of Milton
		Ch (1951) Ufolette of Milton

One of the earliest Belgian Pedigrees
HAMIRETTE OF MILTON (B: Born 21 October 1958)
Breeders M et Mme A. Bellotte

Ch Youbi of Milton	Bambin of Milton	Ch Pitou of Milton 24 September 1931
		Ch Bomba of Milton 12 March 1933
	Ch Ufolette of Milton	Bambin of Milton 29 January 1939
		Quinette of Milton 9 April 1942
Giselle of Milton	Ch Youbi of Milton	Bambin of Milton 29 January 1939
		Ch Ufolette of Milton 15 June 1946
	Ch Ufolette of Milton	Bambin of Milton 29 January 1939
		Quinette of Milton 9 April 1942

Mex Ch DAPPER DAN DE GASCOIGNE (D: Born 27 May 1964)

André de Gascoigne	Jou Jou de Hoop	Galant de Hoop
		Gavotte de Wanarbry
	Hermine de Hoop	Eddy White de Steren Vor
		Etoile de Steren Vor
Lady des Frimoussettes	Amigo Mio D'Egriselles	Xaky de Montessart
		Dolly D'Egriselles
	Houpette des Frimoussettes	Guele de Amour des Frimoussettes
		Bouclette des Frimoussettes

Foremost USA sire of all time
Am Ch CHAMINADE MR BEAU MONDE (D: Born 1970) (p. 25)
Breeder: B. Stubbs, USA. Owners: D. Beauchamp & P. Waterman

Am Ch Cali-Col's Robespierre	Mex Ch Dapper Dan de Gascoigne	André de Gascoigne
		Lady des Frimoussettes
	Lyne of Milton	Helly of Milton
		Hanette of Milton
Am Ch Reenroy's Ami du Kilkanny	Mex Ch Dapper Dan de Gascoigne	André de Gascoigne
		Lady des Frimoussettes
	Little Nell of Cali-Col	Eddy White de Steren Vor
		Nelly of Cali-Col

Am Ch REENROY'S AMI DU KILKANNY (B: Born 11 July 1966)
Breeder: M. Butler, USA. Owner: B. Stubbs

		Jou Jou de Hoop
	André de Gascoigne	
		Hermine de Hoop
Mex Ch Dapper Dan de Gascoigne		
		Amigo Mio d'Egriselles
	Lady des Frimoussettes	
		Houpette des Frimoussettes
		Int Ch Bandit de Steren Vor
	Eddy White de Steren Vor	
		Amy du Lary
Little Nell of Cali-Col		
		Eddy White de Steren Vor
	Nelly of Cali-Col	
		Lassy of Milton

PETIT GALANT DE ST GEORGE (D: Born approx 1967)
Owner: Mrs B Stubbs, USA

		Eddy White de Steren Vor
	Kord du Pic-Four	
		Etoile de Steren Vor
Monsieur Mieux		
		Eddy White de Steren Vor
	Kocenne de Hoop	
		Jaja de Hoop
		Kito of Milton
	Marquis of Milton	
		Giselle of Milton
Cali-Col's Nugget		
		Eddy White de Steren Vor
	Gigi de Hoop	
		Etoile de Steren Vor

Am Ch STARDOM'S ODIN REX JR (Born 12 December 1965)
Breeder: Mrs G. Fournier. Owners: S. Raabe & J. Lande

			Jou Jou de Hoop
		Andre de Gascoigne	
			Hermine de Hoop
	Mex Ch Dapper Dan de Gascoigne		
			Amigo Mio d'Egriselles
		Lady de Frimoussettes	
			Houpette des Frimoussettes
			Ch Youbi of Milton
		Helly of Milton	
			Zoee of Milton
Lyne of Milton			
			Ch Youbi of Milton
		Hanette of Milton	
			Zoee of Milton

———————————

Pedigrees of first Belgian imports
ZETHUS DE CHAPONAY OF TRESILVA (D: Born 10 March 1975)
Breeders: Mr & Mrs Vansteenkiste-Deleu, Belgium. Imported by
  Mrs J. Ransom May 1975   (p. 33)

			Racha de Villa Sainval
		Ugo de Villa Sainval	
			Soraya de Villa Sainval
	Int Ch Xorba de Chaponay		
			Kito of Milton
		Quatna of Milton	
			Giselle of Milton
			Quillan of Milton
		Sapajou de Villa Sainval	
			Raya de Villa Sainval
Veronique de Villa Sainval			
			Qwiky of Milton
		Toscane de Villa Sainval	
			Rebecca de Villa Sainval

ZENA DE CHAPONAY OF TRESILVA (B: Born 3 March 1975)
Breeders: Mr & Mrs Vansteenkiste-Deleu, Belgium. Imported by
Mrs J. Ransom May 1975

Int Ch Bazi v Dandelion

Int Ch Didon v Lindenhaus
- Kin-X-Kaet de Steren Vor
- Cherrie v Lindenhaus

Ala vom Haus Tennstadt
- Int Ch Didon v Lindenhaus
- Diana v Goldfischbrunnen

Xandra de Chaponay

U Trotsky
- Rijou
- Suzy de Villa Sainval

Veronique de Villa Sainval
- Sapajou de Villa Sainval
- Toscane de Villa Sainval

ASTOR DE VILLA SAINVAL OF LITTLECOURT (D: Born 7
April 1976)
Breeder: Mme A. Berben, Belgium. Imported by Mrs M. Harper
& Mrs F. McGregor 1976

Int Ch Xorba de Chaponay

Ugo de Villa Sainval
- Ch Racha de Villa Sainval
- Soraya de Villa Sainval

Quatna of Milton
- Kito of Milton
- Giselle of Milton

Yalta de Villa Sainval

Vim de Villa Sainval
- U Sacha de Villa Sainval
- Toscane de Villa Sainval

Xophie de Villa Sainval
- Sapajou de Villa Sainval
- Raya de Villa Sainval

ASTIR DE CHAPONAY OF TWINLEY (D: Born 23 May 1976)
Breeders: Mr & Mrs Vansteenkiste-Deleu, Belgium. Imported by
Mrs P. Block 1976

Int Ch Xorba de Chaponay	Ugo de Villa Sainval	Int Ch Racha de Villa Sainval
		Soraya de Villa Sainval
	Quatna of Milton	Kito of Milton
		Giselle of Milton
Xcarlet de Villa Sainval	Sapajou de Villa Sainval	Quillan of Milton
		Raya de Villa Sainval
	Uriel de Villa Sainval	Int Ch Racha de Villa Sainval
		Soraya de Villa Sainval

———

HUNTGLEN ZARAH DE CHAPONAY (B: Born 10 October 1975)
Breeders: Mr & Mrs Vansteenkiste-Deleu, Belgium. Imported by
Mrs Harper & Mrs McGregor 1976

Int Ch U Trotsky	Rijou	Unknown
		Unknown
	Suzy de Villa Sainval	Quillan of Milton
		Ominouche
Quatna of Milton	Kito of Milton	Abelli of Milton
		Giselle of Milton
	Giselle of Milton	Ch Youbi of Milton
		Ch Ufolette of Milton

Pedigrees of first litters born in the UK
AUS CH CARLISE CICERO OF TRESILVA (D: Born 3 March 1974)
Breeder: Mrs Sorstein UK. Owner: Mrs J. Ransom   (p. 32)

Rava's Regal Valor of Reenroy
- Ch Stardom's Odin Rex Jr
  - Mex Ch Dapper Dan de Gascoigne
  - Lyne of Milton
- Reenroy's Tina-Tilton
  - Reenroy's Romeo
  - Reenroy's Rebecca

Jenny-Vive de Carlise
- Beaushaun's High Cotton
  - Ch Stardom's Odin.. Rex Jr
  - Beaushaun's Popcorn
- Snowbee de Beaushaun
  - Sledge's Messieur Andre
  - Bo Jill's Trinket de Beaushaun

1st litter born in quarantine 1975
LEANDER SNOW VENTURE (D)
LEANDER SNOW CAROL (B)
LEANDER BEAUMONDE SNOW PUFF (D)
LEANDER ARDEN (D)
(Born 9 September 1975) Breeder: Mrs Streatfield, UK

Am Ch C & D's Beaumonde the Blizzard
- Int Ch C & D's Count Kristopher
  - Peppe de Barnette
  - Quentia of Goldysdale
- Am Ch C & D's Sunbonnet
  - Ch Chaminade Mr Beau Monde
  - Ch C & D's Countess Becky

Am Ch C & D's Beaumonde the Sunflower
- Am Ch Chaminade Mr Beaumonde
  - Ch Cali-Col's Robespierre
  - Ch Reenroy's Ami du Kilkanny
- Am Ch C & D's Countess Becky
  - Peppe de Barnette
  - Quentia of Goldysdale

2nd litter born in quarantine
TWINLEY CHOU CHOU (B)
TWINLEY TIBERIUS (D)
TWINLEY CLAUDIUS (D)
TWINLEY CAESAR (D)
TWINLEY JOSIE POSIE (B)
(Born 12 September 1975) Breeder: Mrs P. Block UK

	Mex Ch Dapper Dan de Gascoigne	André de Gascoigne
Am Ch Cali-Col's Octavius Caesar		Lady des Frimoussettes
	Lyne of Milton	Helly of Milton
		Hanette of Milton
	Dominique Quemby du G.W.	Ombre de la Roche Posay
Cottontops Jolie Ivette of Twinley		Orlanda de la Roche Posay
	Petites Bon Bon de Merle Roui	Ombre de la Roche Posay
		Guex de Merle Roui

Aus Ch JAZZ DE LA BUTHIERE OF LEIJAZULIP (D: Born 17
  October 1974)   (p. 41)
Breeder: Mme Desfarges, France. Imported by Mrs V. Goold &
  Mr D. Chiverton 1975

	Int Ch U Sam de Villa Sainval	Int Ch Racha de Villa Sainval
Int Ch If de la Buthiere		Soraya de Villa Sainval
	Ch Ursee de la Buthiere	Nucky de Wanarbry
		Tarquin de la Buthiere
	Nucky de Wanarbry	Int Ch Jimbo de Steren Vor
Vanda de la Buthiere		Ch Moussia de Wanarbry
	Tornado de Wanarbry	Nucky de Wanarbry
		Rosy de la Roche Posay

INT CH IF DE LA BUTHIERE OF ANTARCTICA (Born 20 May 1973)
Breeder: Mme Desfarges, France. Imported by Mr & Mrs K. Rawlings 1977

Int Ch U Sam de Villa Sainval	Int Ch Racha de Villa Sainval	Kwiki of Milton
		Mowglia of Milton
	Soraya de Villa Sainval	Quillan of Milton
		Mowglia of Milton
Ch Ursee de la Buthiere	Nucky de Wanarbry	Int Ch Jimbo de Steren Vor
		Ch Moussia de Wanarbry
	Tarquin de la Buthiere	Nucky de Wanarbry
		Rosy de la Roche Posay

Pedigree of early French import
LEILAH DE LA BUTHIERE OF LEIJAZULIP (B: Born 5 April 1975)
Breeder: Mme Desfarges, France. Imported by Mrs V. Goold & Mr D. Chiverton 1975

Int Ch U Sam de Villa Sainval	Int Ch Racha de Villa Sainval	Kwiki of Milton
		Mowglia of Milton
	Soraya de Villa Sainval	Quillan of Milton
		Mowglia of Milton
Tornado de Wanarbry	Nucky de Wanarbry	Int Ch Jimbo de Steren Vor
		Ch Moussia de Wanarbry
	Rosy de la Roche Posay	Norman de la Roche Posay
		Loukette de la Roche Posay

Appendix 5
The Kennel Clubs and Bichons Frisés Clubs of the UK

The Kennel Club
1–4 Clarges Street, Piccadilly, London W1Y 8AB

The Scottish Kennel Club
3 Brunswick Place, Edinburgh EH7 5HP

The Welsh Kennel Club
4 Cadwgan Rd, Craig Cefn Park, Swansea, Glam SA6 5AD

The Bichon Frisé Club of Great Britain
Mrs M. Hoad, 8 Sandpiper Walk, Eastbourne, Sussex

The Northern & Midland Bichon Frisé Club
Mrs P. Holbrook-O'Hara, Apple Acre, Lower Heswall, Wirral, Cheshire

The Mid-Eastern Counties Bichon Frisé Club
Mrs L. Fellowes, 14 Swan Street, Sileby, Leics.

The Southern Bichon Frisé Breeders Association
Mrs H. Banfield, Laburnum Lodge, 35 Lower Cippenham Lane, Slough, Berks

Appendix 6
Clubs with which the Kennel Club has reciprocal agreements

Australia
Australian National Kennel Council—Royal Show Grounds,
Ascot Vale Victoria
(Incorporating: The Canine Association of Western Australia
N. Australian Canine Association
The Canine Control Council (Queensland)
Canberra Kennel Association
The Kennel Control Council
Kennel Control Council of Tasmania
New South Wales Canine Control
South Australian Canine Association

Barbados
Barbados Kennel Club, Everton, Dash Valley, St George,
Barbados, West Indies

Belgium
Société Royale Saint-Hubert, Avenue de l'Armée 25, B-1040,
Brussels

Bermuda
The Bermuda Kennel Club Inc., PO Box 1455, Hamilton 5,
Bermuda

Brazil
Brazil Kennel Club, Rua Debret 23, Conj. 1308/10–20030,
Rio de Janeiro

Burma
Burma Kennel Club

Canada
Canadian Kennel Club, 2150 Bloor Street West, Toronto
M6S 1M8, Ontario

Caribbean
The Caribbean Kennel Club, PO Box 737, Port of Spain,
Trinidad

Chile
Kennel Club de Chile, Casilla 1704, Valparsaiso

Colombia
Club Canino Colombiano, Cra. 56 No. 127-A-45, Bogota,
D.E. Colombia, Zona 11

Denmark
Dansk Kennelklub, Parkvej 1, Jersie Strand, 2680, Solrad,
Strand

East Africa
East African Kennel Club, PO Box 14223, St Andrews
Church, Nyerere Road, Nairobi, Kenya

Finland
Soumen Kennelliitto-Finska Kennelklubben, Kamreerintie 8,
SE 022770, Espoo

France
Société Centrale Canine, 215 Rue St Denis, 75093 Paris,
Cedex 02

Germany
Verband fur das Deutsche Hundewesen (VDH), Hoher Wall
20, D460, Dortmund

Guernsey
Guernsey Dog Club, Le Hurel Farm, St Saviours, Guernsey,
Channel Islands

Holland
Raad van Beheer op Kynologisch Gebied in Nederland, Emmalaan 16, Amsterdam

Hong Kong
Hong Kong Kennel Club, 3rd Floor, 28B Stanley Street, Hong Kong

India
Kennel Club of India, 9 Balar Kalir Nilayam Avenue, off Ritherdon Road, Purasawalkam, Madras 600007

Ireland
Irish Kennel Club, 23 Earlsfort Terrace, Dublin 2

Italy
Ente Nazionale Della Cinofilia Italiana, Viale Premuda, 21 Milan

Jamaica
The Jamaica Kennel Club, 117 Old Hope Road, Kingston 6, Jamaica, West Indies

Jersey
Jersey Dog Club, Toneham Lodge, Princes Tower Road, St Saviour, Jersey, Channel Islands

Malaysia
Malaysian Kennel Association, No. 8, Jalan Tun Mohd Faud Dua, Taman Tun Dr Ismail, Kuala Lumpur

Malta, GC
Main Kennel Club, c/o Msida Youth Centre, 15 Rue d'Argens Str, Msida

Monaco
Société Canine de Monaco, Palais des Congres, Avenue d'Ostende, Monte Carlo

Nepal
Nepal Kennel Club, PO Box 653, Kathmandu

New Zealand
New Zealand Kennel Club, Private Bag, Porirua

Norway
Norsk Kennelklub, Nils Hansens Vei 20, Box 163-Bryn 0611, Oslo 6

Pakistan
The Kennel Club of Pakistan

Portugal
Cluba Portuguese de Canicultura, Praca D Joao da Camara 4–3, Lisbon 2

Singapore
The Singapore Kennel Club, 170 Upper Bukit Timah Road, 12.02 Singapore 2158

South Africa
Kennel Union of South Africa, 6th Floor, Bree Castle, 68 Bree Street, Cape Town 8001, S. Africa, Box 2659, Cape Town 8000

Spain
Real Sociedad Central de Fomento de las Razas en Espana, Los Madrazo 20, Madrid 14

Sweden
Svenska Kennelklubben, Norrbyvagan 30, Box 11043, 161 11 Bromma

Switzerland
Schweizerische Kynologische Gesellschaft, Falkenplatz 11, 3012, Bern

Uruguay
Kennel Club Uruguayo, Avda, Uruguay 864, Montevideo

USA
American Kennel Club, 51 Madison Avenue, New York, NY 10010

Zambia
Kennel Association of Zambia, PO Box 22021, Kitwe

Zimbabwe
The Zimbabwe Kennel Club, PO Box BE 81, Belvedere

Appendix 7
The Kennel Club Junior Organisation

This organisation, founded to promote sportsmanship, courtesy, loyalty and self discipline among young devotees of the dog, offers young people between the ages of 8 and 18 the opportunity, whether they own a dog or not, to join in the various interesting activities held each year.

Members of the KCJO enjoy many activities connected with the dog world, including visits to shows, dog training centres, dog trials, local kennels, dog sanctuaries and various other activities. It is also possible to learn about the care and training of the dog from experts such as veterinary surgeons, training instructors and, of particular interest to the Bichon Frisé owner, canine beauticians.

During the holiday periods agility and obedience competitions are held, with an annual quiz competition to find the winning regional team. Every year many of the great Championship Shows schedule KCJO Any Variety (any Breed) Stakes Classes which only members can enter. One other interesting yearly occasion is the competition for 'Junior of the Year' based on an original written and pictorial 'Project and Diary of all the Canine Activities of the Year'. The winner of this competition is awarded the Shaun McAlpine Memorial Trophy, which is normally presented at Crufts by HRH Prince Michael of Kent.

Application for membership or information about the KCJO should be made to the Kennel Club.

Appendix 8
Glossary of Canine Terminology

AFFIX   A registered name used when registering a dog at the Kennel Club
ALMOND EYE   The eye set in an almond-shaped surround
ANORCHID   Male animal without testicles
ANUS   Anterior opening under the tail
ANGULATION   Angle formed by the bones, mainly shoulder, stifle and hock

BALANCE   Correctly proportioned animal, with one part in regard to another
BARREL-RIBS   Rounded ribs
BITCH   A female
BRISKET   The forepart of the body below the chest
BROOD BITCH   A bitch used for breeding
BUTTERFLY NOSE   Parti-colour nose, spotted with flesh colour
BRACE   Two dogs of the same breed

CANINES   Long pointed teeth, two upper and two lower next to incisors
CARPALS   Wrist bones
CASTRATE   To surgically remove the testes
CHALLENGE CERTIFICATE   An award by the Kennel Club for the best exhibit of each sex in the breed at a Championship Show, which in the opinion of the judge is worthy of the title of Champion
CHAMPION   A dog which has won three Challenge Certificates under three different judges
CHINA EYE   A clear blue eye
CLOSE-COUPLED   A dog comparatively short between ribs and pelvis
CONFORMATION   The structure and form of the dog's framework
COW-HOCKS   Hocks turned inwards towards one another

CROUP The back, from the front of the pelvis to the root of the tail

CRYPTORCHID A male with one or both testicles retained in the abdominal cavity

CULL To eliminate unwanted puppies

DAM Mother of puppies

DEWCLAW Extra claw on inside of front and back legs, should be removed from the Bichon Frisé

DEWLAP Loose pendulous skin under the throat

DOUBLE COAT Undercoat with a longer top coat

DRIVE Good thrust of rear quarters

FEMUR The bone between hip and stifle

FOREARM Front legs between elbow and wrist

GESTATION The time between conception and birth, usually 59–63 days

HACKNEY ACTION The front feet lifted high

HALOES Dark pigmentation over or around the eyes usually at the inner corners on a Bichon Frisé.

HAW The third eyelid at the inside corner of the eye

HEAT An alternative word for 'season' or 'Oestrus'

HEIGHT Usually measured from withers to ground

HOCK The lower joint of the hind legs

HUMERUS Bone of the upper arm

INBREEDING The mating of closely related animals

INCISORS Upper and lower front teeth between the canines, 6 in the upper jaw and 6 in the lower

INTERNATIONAL CHAMPION A dog that has gained its title in more than one country

LAYBACK The angle of the shoulder blade compared with the vertical

LEATHER The ear flap

LEVEL BITE The upper and lower teeth meeting edge to edge

LINE-BREEDING The mating of dogs with a common ancestor

LOADED Superfluous muscle

LOIN Either side of the vertebral column between the last rib and the hip bone

MAIDEN   An unmated bitch: or in show classification a dog or bitch that has never won a 1st prize

METATARSALS   Bones between the hock joint and the foot

MONORCHID   A male animal with only one testicle in the scrotum

MOLARS   The back teeth: 6 in the lower jaw and 4 in the upper

OCCIPUT   The highest point at the rear of the skull

OESTRUS   The period of menstrual flow and the time for mating

OUT AT ELBOW   Elbows turning out from the body

OVERSHOT   Front teeth (incisors) of the upper jaw overlapping the lower teeth without touching

PACING   The left foreleg and left hindleg move together followed by the right foreleg and right hindleg

PASTERN   The area between the wrist above and the digits below

PATELLA   The knee cap; part of the stifle joint

PIGEON-TOED   Forefeet inclined inwards

PIGMENT   Colour of skin

PLUME   Long hair hanging from the tail

PREFIX   *see* Affix

PREMOLAR   The teeth between the canines and the molars: 8 in top jaw and 8 in the lower jaw

PUPPY   A dog up to 12 months of age

PUPPY CLASS   Classes for puppies between 6 and 12 months old

QUALITY   Refinement

RING TAIL   Carried up: almost in a circle

ROACH BACK   A convex curvature of the back

SCISSOR BITE   Upper teeth closely overlap and touch the lower teeth

SECOND THIGH   The part of the hindquarters from stifle to hock

SIRE   A dog's male parent

SLAB SIDED   Flat ribs

SNIPY   Muzzle pointed and weak

SPAY   To surgically remove the ovaries and uterus to prevent conception

SPLAYED   Flat feet

SPRING   The roundness of the ribs

STANDARD   A word picture of a breed

STERNUM   Breast bone

STIFLE   Knee

STOP   Indentation between the eyes

STUD BOOK   A Kennel Club record of winning dogs, used for breeding purposes

STRAIGHT IN SHOULDER   Shoulder blades insufficently laid back

THIGH   Hindquarters from hip to stifle

THROATINESS   An excess of skin under the throat

TOPKNOT   The long hair on the head

TOPLINE   The outline of a dog from withers to tail set

TOY DOG   A small dog, ie a lap dog

TUCK-UP   An upward curve from rib end to waist

TYPE   Qualities that distinguish a breed

UNDERCOAT   A dense soft short coat concealed by a longer top coat

UNDERSHOT   The lower front teeth (incisors) overlapping the front teeth of the upper jaw

UPPER ARM   The humerus or bone of the foreleg between shoulder blade and forearm

WEAVING   The crossing of the front or hindlegs when in action

WHELP   An unweaned puppy

WITHERS   The union between the shoulder blade and the thoracic vertebrae; located just behind the base of the neck. The height of a dog is measured at this point

WRY MOUTH   Lower jaw not in line with upper jaw

Appendix 9
Glossary of Canine Abbreviations

AI	Artificial insemination
AKC	American Kennel Club
ALSH	Annexe Livre Saint-Hubert
ANKC	Australian National Kennel Club
ARAF	Active registration applied for
AOC	Any other colour
AVNSC	Any variety not separately classified
B	Bitch
BFCofGB	Bichon Frisé Club of Great Britain
BIS	Best in Show
BOB	Best of Breed
BOS	Best Opposite Sex
Br	Breeder
BVA	British Veterinary Association
CAC	Certificat d'aptitude au Championnat de Beauté
CACIB	Certificat d'aptitude au Championnat Internationale de Beauté
CC	Challenge Certificate
CD	Companion Dog
CDX	Companion Dog Excellent
CKC	Canadian Kennel Club
D	Dog (male)
ENCI	Ente Nazionale della Cinofilia Italiana
FCI	Fédération Cynologique Internationale
FT Ch	Field Trial Champion
IKC	Irish Kennel Club
Int Ch	International Champion

Ir Ch	Irish Champion
JKC	Jersey Kennel Club
KC	Kennel Club
KCJO	Kennel Club Junior Organisation
LKA	Ladies Kennel Association
LOF	Livre des Originés Francais
LOSH	Livre Originés Saint-Hubert
NAF	Name applied for
N&MBFC	Northern and Midland Bichon Frisé Club
OB CH	Obedience Champion
P	Puppy (a dog under 12 months)
RI	Registre Initial
RES CC	Reserve Challenge Certificate
S	Sieger (German Champion)
SBFBA	Southern Bichon Frisé Breeders Association
SKC	Scottish Kennel Club
TAF	Transfer applied for
WELKS	West of England Ladies Kennel Society
WKC	Welsh Kennel Club
WS	Weltsieger (World Champion, Germany)

Bibliography

One of the most valuable sources of information on all aspects of the dog are the numerous books written about their care, breeding and welfare. Many of the books listed below although not specifically on the Bichon Frisé give us the opportunity to learn and profit from some of the greatest authorities past and present.

Genetics of the Dog: Malcolm B. Willis, H. F. & G. Witherby, 1989

The Theory and Practice of Breeding to Type C. J. Davies, 'Our Dogs'

Practical Dog Breeding & Genetics E. Franklin, Popular Dogs, 1961

Dogs & I Harding Cox, Hutchinson, 1920

Conformation of the Dog R. H. Smythe, Faber & Faber, 1957

Understanding your Dog Michael Fox, Coward, McCann & Geoghegan, 1972

Dog Steps R. P. Elliott, Howell, NY, 1973

The Bichon Frisé Today R. G. Beauchamp, Rohman, USA, 1982

This is the Bichon Frisé Bearley & Nicholas, TFH, 1973

Dogs in Britain C. L. Hubbard, Macmillan, 1948

Dogs Through History Maxwell Riddle, Delinger, USA, 1987

All about Mating, Whelping and Weaning David Cavill, Pelham, 1980

Take Them Round Please Tom Horner, Faber & Faber, 1975

Man Meets Dog Konrad Lorenz, Methuen, 1954

About Our Dogs A. Croxton Smith, Ward Lock, 1931

Breeding from Your Poodle Sheldon & Lockwood, Foyles, 1963

Training Dogs Konrad Most, Popular Dogs

Canine Terminology Harold R. Spira, Harper & Row

Picture Credits

The author and publisher wish to thank the owners who have kindly supplied photographs of their dogs. The photographs were taken as follows: Mr Beaumonde the Huckster by MikRon; Tiopepi Mad Louie at Pamplona, Caywood Little Jack Horner and Orpheus Orion of Atroya by Hartley; Sulyka Snoopy by Sally-Anne Thompson; Leijazulip Jazz of Zudiki by M. Trafford; Jaqueline Leijazulip at Tresilva by Foyle; Melsel Cracklin Rosie by David Freeman; Bumbleridge Overture at Rossage by Des Cox; Bobander Toot the Flute and Edelweiss Ebony Eyes by Russell Fine Art; Emmrill Snow Pipit, Roushka's Song and Dance, Roushka's Dancemaster, Sibon Sloane Ranger at Pamplona, Rossage Silver Ghost and Leander Snow Cat by David Dalton; Ligray Mr Beau Geste by Martin Leigh; Melsel Kiss Me Kate by Diane Pearce and Sulyka Puzzle by Thomas Fall. Other pictures by Marc Henrie.